Great Women Teachers

ALICE FLEMING

Great Women Teachers

J. B. LIPPINCOTT COMPANY

Philadelphia and New York

CONTENTS

Great Women Teachers

ONE

❧ *Emma Hart Willard*

Have you ever seen a determined woman? Florence Nightingale was one; so was Clara Barton; and, although many people do not know it, Emma Willard was another one.

It is not always easy to figure out how a determined woman gets that way but Emma Willard began by being a determined little girl. Oddly enough, however, one of the first things she was determined to do was to stay home from school.

Emma was born in Berlin, Connecticut, in 1787. In those years just after the American Revolution, few states had anything resembling a public school system. What schools there were generally limited their enrollment to boys. Girls could pick up a smattering of learning at home—just enough reading to help them get through their prayer-books on Sunday.

Connecticut, though, had been one of the first colonies to set up public grammar schools and during the summer months when the boys were busy on the farms, girls were allowed to attend. Gradually they began to go in the winter time as well.

Emma went to the district school at Worthington Center. There in the weather-beaten old one-room schoolhouse, she learned to read and do sums and to practice her penmanship in her brown paper covered copy book, writing with homemade ink and the goose quill that the schoolmaster had sharpened into a pen for her.

Then one afternoon, Emma's father, Samuel Hart, came home with the news that a brand new academy was to open in Worthington Center.

"Dr. Thomas Miner who is a graduate of Yale University will be the teacher," he said, "and they are going to enroll girls as well as boys. That means Emma will have a chance to continue the work she is doing at the district school."

Ordinarily, Emma Hart would have been thrilled at the prospect of attending the new academy but now she was not so sure. The school was scheduled to open the very week she was planning to visit her married sister, Mary Lee, whose daughters were her favorite playmates.

"I really don't want to start school," Emma whispered to her sister Nancy that evening as the two girls snuggled beneath the eiderdown quilts in their high four-poster bed. "Do you think Mother and Father will be angry if I go to visit Mary instead?"

"I don't know," murmured Nancy sleepily, "why don't you ask them?"

"That's just what I'll do," Emma said slipping out from under the covers and padding down the hall to her parents' room.

"Mother, Father," she called.

"Come in, Emma," Mrs. Hart said. "What on earth is the matter?"

"Don't you think it is unfair to send people to school who do not wish to be educated?" Emma demanded.

"Did you wake us up in the middle of the night just to ask us that?" Samuel Hart wanted to know.

"Well," Emma blurted out, "I was just wondering if I could go to visit Mary instead of starting school next week."

"Why, Emma," Lydia Hart said, "I thought you would be anxious to continue your studies."

Samuel Hart sat up in bed, the light from Emma's candle flickering across his kindly face.

"I don't believe in forcing education on someone who can neither absorb it nor appreciate it," he said decisively. "You may go to Mary's if you wish. Now let us all go back to sleep."

So while Nancy Hart washed and ironed her calico school dresses, Emma packed her valise for the trip to Mary Lee's house in Kensington.

When she returned from her visit the following week, however, Emma was not at all sure she had made the right decision. Nancy had a new geography book.

"We are learning all about the continents and the oceans," she told Emma, "and Dr. Miner has the most wonderful maps and charts . . . he is going to teach us history and mathematics and . . ."

Emma could stand it no longer. "Mother, Mother," she called as she darted down the stairs to the kitchen.

Mother was busy at the spinning wheel and before she could even ask what the trouble was, Emma announced breathlessly, "Mother, I am going to school tomorrow!"

"But, Emma," Mrs. Hart replied, "I thought you had made up your mind not to be educated, and besides your clothes are not in order, and it will appear odd for you to enter school on Saturday."

"But I must," Emma insisted, still struggling to regain her breath, "I . . . absolutely . . . MUST!"

The following morning the determined young scholar was enrolled at the new academy.

"You will have to study by yourself for a few weeks," Dr. Miner told her, "until you have caught up with the rest of the class."

Emma Hart made up her mind not to lag behind for long. One night when her sister Lydia was having a party, she even took her books and went outside in the bitter cold to study by the light of the winter moon.

There she sat, huddled on a tree stump a few yards from the kitchen door, her woolen cloak wrapped snugly around her shoulders and her copy of Morse's Geography hugged close to her chest.

It was dark and cold out there in the yard and occasionally the weary student would glance back over her shoulder at the lighted windows of the three-story brown farmhouse where she had been born. Inside, some of the girls were singing and their voices drifted out over the clear night air. Emma thought of how warm and cozy it must be in there by the fire. They would probably be drinking cider and there might even be a taffy pull.

"But this is more important," Emma reminded herself sternly as she turned her back on the farmhouse and looking away towards the shadowy outline of the Connecticut hills, attacked her geography lesson once more.

It was close to nine o'clock when Emma Hart finally closed her book and returned to the house. Her sister's company had long since gone, and Samuel Hart and his wife Lydia were sitting before the kitchen hearth.

"You must be frozen, Emma," Mrs. Hart said, glancing up from her knitting. "Couldn't you have studied in here by the fire?"

Emma shook her head. "Lydia had guests in the parlor," she said, "and I know I would have been tempted to join in their fun."

Samuel Hart looked up from his book. "You mean you prefer geography to parties?" he exclaimed in mock astonishment. "I thought you were the girl who did not want to be educated."

"I've changed my mind," the pretty teenager replied with a smile, "and now I won't stop working until I'm the most educated girl in Connecticut!"

Three days after she entered Dr. Miner's school, Emma Hart had caught up with the rest of the class and it was not much longer before she surpassed them all. Recognizing her abilities, Thomas Miner encouraged her to write and think clearly. In later life, Emma often talked about the two years that she had spent at the Berlin Academy.

"I believe," she said, "that no better instruction was given to girls in any school at that time in our country."

Emma was seventeen when she left Dr. Miner's classes at Worthington Center to teach at the children's school in the village.

"Little did I realize then," she once remarked, "that I was undertaking a career which would last with only slight interruption for the next forty years!"

That first day at the district school, however, almost made her give up in despair. The class she was assigned to teach had been in charge of a woman who made no attempt to enforce discipline. The school itself was situated on the main street facing the Hartford and New Haven turnpike and the children spent more time admiring the passing traffic than they did at their lessons. Not content with the view from the window, the more adventurous ones would often saunter outside while class was in session. A few even ran off to play in the mulberry grove that surrounded the building on three sides.

As soon as Emma had taken her place at the desk, she realized that she was about to face the longest morning of her life.

"Goodness knows how I shall ever survive," she thought grimly, but aloud she said, "Now, children, let us start working in our copy books."

Three or four girls reached for their books but most of

the class ignored Emma completely and went right on doodling on their slates. One boy wandered over to the door to watch a horse and carriage and another jumped on a bench in the back of the classroom, leaped out the window and went tearing through the mulberry grove.

"Children, please!" Emma said, vainly clapping her hands to restore order.

When it was finally time to dismiss the class for lunch, the new teacher sank wearily back into her chair. She did not even have the strength to smile when Mrs. Peck, the woman who had recommended her for the teaching position, stopped by to see how things were going.

"It was a dreadful morning," Emma moaned. "I don't know how I can teach these children anything. They simply will not obey. Talking does no good. Reasoning is even worse."

"Those children need a sound spanking," said Mrs. Peck. "That will show them who's in charge."

Emma was horrified. "I cannot," she said. "I never struck a child in my life."

"It is the only way," Mrs. Peck replied firmly. "You must."

The next morning as Emma faced her unruly class once more, Mrs. Peck's young son Jesse entered the room with a bundle of five rods. "My mother thought you might want these," he said.

In desperation Emma picked one of the sticks up and showed it to the class. "You see this," she said, "I shall use it if I have to."

For awhile a hush fell over the class. Then one young man rose defiantly from his seat. Emma grabbed him firmly, spanked his bottom with one of her rods and returned him to his chair.

"You boys and girls do not seem to understand that I am here to do you good," Emma told them. "Learning will make you useful and happy citizens but I can never teach you anything if you do not mind."

Most of the boys and girls began to pay attention but a few were still determined to test the new teacher. By now Emma had no qualms. She used her rods for every infraction and the following day, the entire class filed quietly into the classroom and meekly obeyed her every request.

Emma soon had her boys and girls hard at work and it was not long before the school was the admiration of the neighborhood; but the youthful schoolmistress was very happy that never again in her teaching career did she have to resort to physical punishment to obtain order in a classroom.

Emma Hart fared so well at the children's school that she was invited to take charge of the Berlin Academy which she herself had attended under Dr. Thomas Miner. Still determined to be the most educated girl in Connecticut, she also took time between terms to return to school herself. One year she studied art with the Misses Patten in Hartford and the following year she enrolled at Mrs. Royse's school where the curriculum included reading, writing, arithmetic, geography and French as well as such ladylike subjects as dancing, drawing, painting and needle-work.

A girl of college age today would probably laugh at such simple courses but in 1806, this was considered a superior education for a young lady. Most girls never went beyond the district school, if indeed they were lucky enough to go that far.

Shortly after Emma Hart's twentieth birthday, she learned of an opening for a teacher at the female academy in Middlebury, Vermont. She applied for it and was hired at once.

Emma found Middlebury a lively town. After a busy day in the classroom, she often spent her evenings at concerts, lectures and parties. She wrote to her parents, "I go to school generally before nine, and stay till one; come home, snatch my dinner, go again, and stay till almost sundown; come home, and dress in a great hurry to go abroad, get home about ten, fatigued enough to go to bed, and lie till seven the next morning, with hardly time enough to mend my stockings."

Vermont may have been livelier than Connecticut, but it was also colder. Emma often had to trudge through heavy snowdrifts to reach the academy. And inside the white frame building the temperature was usually not much improved. There was only one small fireplace at the far end of the room and when the cold became completely unbearable, Emma would line all of her pupils up for a country dance.

"It is the only way to keep from freezing to death," she told them. "Our lessons can wait for awhile."

Some of the girls would sing and the rest would clap hands while they skipped back and forth, curls bouncing and skirts flying until they were warm enough to return to their work.

Like any other attractive young woman of twenty, Emma loved going to parties and dances. She was particularly impressed with the young men she met in Middlebury. "The beaux here," she wrote to her mother, "are, the greater part of them, men of collegiate education."

Intelligent, well-educated and mature beyond her years, it was only natural for Emma Hart to enjoy the company of men somewhat older than herself. One of her acquaintances was Dr. John Willard, a widower with four children who had given up a successful medical practice in order to participate more actively in the business and political affairs of the state of Vermont.

Dr. Willard soon began calling regularly on the young teacher and it was not long before he asked her to become his wife. They were married in Middlebury on August 10, 1809, and Emma Hart Willard abandoned her classroom to become the mistress of her husband's imposing brick home on Main Street. A year later she was blessed with the arrival of a son who was christened John Hart Willard.

Busy as she was running her household and tending her small son, Emma Willard never lost her interest in education. She read and studied by herself and when Dr. Willard's nephew boarded with them while attending Middlebury

College, she pored over all his textbooks and asked endless questions about his courses of study.

The more she learned of how a men's school operated, the more Emma realized that something must be done to provide equal educational opportunities for women.

"Female academies are nothing but finishing schools," she told her husband. "It seems to me that the women of this country have a right to some real honest-to-goodness education!"

It might have taken years for the women of the United States to get that education had not John Willard come home one day with some alarming news.

"The State Bank has been robbed," he announced. "Twenty-eight thousand dollars is missing."

Many people thought that the bank's board of directors, of which Dr. Willard was a member, were somehow responsible for the theft and although the directors were subsequently proved innocent, they were forced, at the time, to make restitution for the stolen money. John Willard lost most of his savings and was forced to mortgage his property as well.

Emma Willard cheerfully adjusted to the more modest circumstances in which they were forced to live but she was also determined to relieve her husband of at least part of his financial burden.

"John," she told him, "I would like to open a school for girls right here in this house."

Dr. Willard would not hear of it. "I will not allow my wife to support me," he said flatly.

"But, John," Emma pleaded, "you know how much I enjoy teaching. And besides, I've been praying for a chance to put some of my educational theories into practice."

John Willard must have seen the determined gleam in his wife's eyes. "All right, Emma," he finally agreed, "if it will make you happy."

The new school opened in the spring of 1814. Music, drawing and penmanship were included in the curriculum but Emma Willard's girls—some seventy of them—also studied higher mathematics, languages, philosophy and history. To the horror of the faculty, Emma even asked if her students might sit in on some of the classes at Middlebury College.

"We must refuse," the president of the school told her. "Having girls attending college classes would create an unfortunate precedent."

Undaunted, Emma devised her own college courses and at the end of the term, she invited the entire faculty to listen to her girls recite at their final examinations.

"You see, gentlemen," she told the astonished professors, "my girls are every bit as capable of grasping difficult subjects as your young men."

Encouraged by the progress she was making with her own school in Middlebury, Emma set to work drawing up a Plan for Improving Female Education.

"Maybe this will convince people that girls should be allowed in our high schools and colleges," she told her husband.

In 1818, Emma Willard sent a copy of her manuscript to Governor DeWitt Clinton of New York. Impressed with the plan she had outlined, the governor invited her to visit the capital at Albany to make an appeal before the New York State Legislature.

Emma's speech to the lawmakers was so impressive that a group of Waterford citizens promptly invited her to start a female seminary in their community. Emma agreed and the state legislature granted a charter to the Waterford Academy for Young Ladies, the first official measure recognizing the right of women to be educated. To Emma's delight, the legislature also decided to allow the academy to share in the state's educational funds which before that had been allotted only to boys' schools.

Emma Willard's battle for equal education for women was by no means over, however. While many prominent citizens praised her Plan, many others decried it. "If women start reading books and studying mathematics," people asked, "who will bake the bread and mend the clothes?"

"Next thing you know, they'll be educating the cows," snorted one crusty old farmer.

Spectators stared in disbelief when Mary Cramer, one of the pupils at the Waterford Academy, recited theorems in geometry during a public examination.

"She must have memorized them," they decided. "No woman could possibly understand geometry."

Even some of the legislators who had granted a charter

to the academy began to have second thoughts about the idea. At the next session they voted to discontinue the state funds for the school.

The decision was a bitter blow for Emma. She refused to charge exorbitant fees yet she could not afford to run the academy without financial assistance.

"But I will not give up," Emma declared. "There must be some way to continue my work."

Less than a week later, she received a note from a group of influential men in Troy, New York. "Won't you move your school to our city?" they wanted to know. "We will be happy to see that you receive whatever funds are necessary to continue its operation."

"It seems now," Emma wrote to her mother, "as if providence has opened the way for the permanent establishment of the school on the plan which I wish to execute."

Emma Willard's Female Seminary opened in Troy in the spring of 1821. Of the ninety young ladies enrolled at the school, twenty-nine came from the town itself; the rest came from other parts of the state, from Vermont, Massachusetts, Connecticut and even from as far as Ohio, South Carolina and Georgia.

Dr. Willard, who had been a great help to Emma in organizing the seminary, continued to serve as its business manager, thereby freeing Emma to concentrate on the curriculum and the students.

One thing she was particularly strict about was housekeeping. Boarders were expected to keep their rooms in order at all times. Dress was another matter not to be over-looked.

"Mrs. Willard wishes the dress of her pupils during school hours to consist of calico, gingham or crape, made in plain style," read the school catalog. "Parents and guardians are earnestly requested not to furnish their daughters or wards with expensive laces, jewelry or any other needless articles of apparel nor to leave with them the control of money."

Emma Willard's greatest concern, however, was the education of her students. She was particularly unhappy with the textbooks they were using. Dull and ponderous, they explained little of the subject matter and included instead endless pages of memory work. Not surprisingly the girls often wrote on the flyleaves:

> *Some books are to be tasted*
> *Some chewed and digested*
> *Some read and detested*
> *Such is this!*

Determined to remedy the situation, Emma Willard in 1822 collaborated with William Channing Woodbridge on a geography textbook that was soon being used in schools all over the country. This was the first of several books on which she worked and which eventually provided her with a substantial income for the rest of her life.

As important as good books, however, were good teach-ers.

"It is my hope," Emma Willard told her students, "that

after leaving the Seminary, you will not spend your days in idleness, but will consider entering the teaching profession, a highly proper calling for young ladies and one for which your training here at the Seminary has properly prepared you."

A certificate signed with Emma Willard's name soon became the highest recommendation any teacher could have and Emma prided herself that she had educated two hundred young teachers at her seminary before even one was graduated from a public normal school.

Nor did she limit her training only to daughters of upper class families. Any girl who wished to become a teacher was accepted at the Troy Female Seminary without charge. Many received clothing and pocket money as well. So anxious was Emma Willard to provide good teachers for the nation's schools that it has been estimated that she gave away some $75,000 worth of scholarships.

After John Willard's death in 1825, Emma continued her work alone. The Troy Female Seminary became famous for the high calibre of education it offered and Emma Willard herself was acclaimed as a pioneer in the field of higher education for women. She traveled widely, lecturing on her work and encouraging the establishment of more female seminaries all over the country.

In 1838 she retired as headmistress and turned the school management over to her son John and his wife Sarah, who had once been a scholarship student at the seminary.

Emma Willard had no intention of giving up the fight for better education, however. Returning to her native state of Connecticut, she assisted State School Superintendent Henry Barnard in his struggles to achieve all the things that are today taken for granted in every school system—good textbooks, school libraries and competent teachers.

In later years, Emma Willard made her home at the Troy Female Seminary where she died quietly in 1870 only two months after her eighty-third birthday. The Seminary was officially renamed the Emma Willard School in 1910 but the determined lady who had founded it would have been even more pleased to know that by that time her dream of equal education for women had finally become a reality.

TWO
ꙍ《 Mary Lyon

In a peaceful corner of the Mount Holyoke College campus in South Hadley, Massachusetts, stands a simple grave. Its marker says: "MARY LYON, The Founder of Mount Holyoke Female Seminary, and for twelve years its Principal; a teacher for thirty-five years, and of more than three thousand pupils. Born, February 28, 1797. Died, March 5, 1849."

The stonecutter who so carefully chiseled these words into the fine Italian marble probably knew very little about the woman whose monument he inscribed, nor could he have foreseen that her Female Seminary would eventually be numbered among the foremost women's colleges in the country and that she herself would be acclaimed as one of America's outstanding educators.

Even Mary Lyon never imagined such a future for herself during her girlhood on her father's farm near Buckland, Massachusetts. It was not a very large or prosperous farm but Mary loved the roses and peonies that grew in its carefully tended flower garden, the apples and peaches plucked from its fruitful orchards and the wild strawberries that dotted its grassy hillsides.

There were seven young Lyons and Mary often said that she had come from a family where there was "just *enough* food and no more." Mr. Lyon died when Mary was only six but Mary's mother, with the help of her children, continued to run her husband's farm. Each child, as soon as he was old enough to walk, was expected to take on his share of the chores. The boys worked in the fields and tended the horses and cows; the girls spun and sewed and cooked and cleaned, and on winter Sundays, the whole family huddled together in the old-fashioned horsedrawn sleigh and glided across the snow-crusted path to church.

Sometimes, during the summer when the long days were just beginning to dwindle into dusk, Mary would slip away from her spinning wheel and scramble up the rocky hillside to her favorite hiding place. "The top of the hill," she liked to call it, but often it seemed more like the top of the world. Stretched out on a huge rock perched at the crest of one of the steepest hills in Buckland, Mary could see the entire valley spread out beneath her—the farms, so carefully marked out and planted, the houses, gleaming white against the dark green fields, the road to church, like a fat brown snake winding through the trees.

While Mary was still quite young, her mother decided to enroll her at the district school. "We must learn to work with our minds as well as with our hands," Mrs. Lyon liked to remind her busy children.

The new pupil soon proved to be the star of the little schoolhouse. She quickly mastered reading and writing and when the class was assigned a lesson in grammar, she whizzed through the entire book in four days. "But that is our work for the whole year," her astonished teacher exclaimed. "If you keep on at this rate, Mary, you will be conducting the class and I will be sitting on the benches with the students!"

By the time she was twelve years old, Mary Lyon had made up her mind to become a teacher. "I think that's a wonderful idea," said Mrs. Lyon when Mary announced her decision one evening at the dinner table.

"A teacher?" piped up one of the younger members of the family. "I never heard of a lady teacher. Aren't all of the teachers men?"

"They are now," Mrs. Lyon said, "but that does not mean they must always be. Mary is a bright girl and I think she would make an excellent teacher."

Mary Lyon's determination to pursue a career immediately set her apart from the other young girls in Buckland. "Only boys decide what they are going to do in life," one of her schoolmates reminded her primly.

"But that doesn't seem fair," Mary replied. "Why should a dozen different boys choose a dozen different jobs—carpenters, lawyers, ministers, farmers—while every girl must grow up to be exactly the same as every other girl?"

"My mother says that girls were made to be wives and mothers," her young friend snapped, "and if the good Lord wanted them to be anything else, he certainly would have given them more brains."

At this, Mary laughed out loud. "Girls have plenty of brains," she said, "and that is why I want to be a teacher— so I can show them how to use them."

Sometimes, though, when she sat by herself on top of her hill, Mary wondered if she would ever really be able to make her dream come true. "A good teacher needs a good education," she reminded herself, "and a good education costs money."

Though she was still only in her teens, Mary began working as an assistant teacher in the district school. Her salary was seventy-five cents a week. "At least it is a beginning," she told herself. "Perhaps in a few years time I will have enough money saved to enable me to continue my studies."

Shortly after Mary had taken on her first job, she found herself offered a second one. Mrs. Lyon remarried and moved away with her new husband and the younger children. Mary's older brother, it was decided, would keep the farm in Buckland. "I would be most grateful," he told his sister, "if you would stay and run the house for me. I can only pay you a dollar a week but . . ."

"A dollar a week!" Mary cried, throwing her arms around the lanky young farmer. "Why that is marvelous! I'll stay until you have found a wife to replace me."

Mary's battered old leather purse soon grew fat with the coins that she so faithfully hoarded from her two weekly salaries. "We are getting there," she would whisper hopefully, patting its bulging sides, "slowly but surely."

It was more than a year before Mary had finally saved enough for her tuition at Sanderson Academy in nearby Ashfield, Massachusetts. Her brother had selected a bride by then and no longer needed her help. "Don't ever forget," he told his sister, "that this is your home. You must feel free to come and stay with us whenever you can."

The other students at the Sanderson Academy were mostly young ladies from well-to-do families. They took one look at their new classmate and burst into giggles. Her hands were rough from housework, her dark hair was pulled back in a plain bun and her blue homespun dress hung shapelessly from her slender shoulders. "It looks just like a flour sack," one of her schoolmates whispered cruelly.

There were no more insults, however, when the new pupil began to work. After only one day of study, she had memorized her entire Latin grammar and she soon topped the class in every other subject as well. "Positively amazing," her teachers proclaimed.

"Not at all," Mary Lyon told them. "My means are so limited that my stay in this academy will be short so I must make the most possible of the opportunity."

At the end of the term, the principal of the school called her into his office. "Miss Lyon," he said, "you are one of the most extraordinary students it has ever been my pleasure to know. I insist that you stay on with us for another semester."

"I am sorry, sir," the young woman replied, "but I cannot possibly afford it."

"Miss Lyon," the principal informed her gently, "I am inviting you to be our guest."

So Mary Lyon stayed on in Ashfield and completed a second term at Sanderson Academy. Her quick mind and diligent attention to her studies continued to amaze her teachers.

"I should like to see what she could do at college," one of them confided to a colleague.

"Any college would be fortunate to get her," the man replied. "What a shame she isn't a boy."

After graduating from Sanderson Academy, Mary accepted a teaching position in Shelburne Falls, not far from her brother's farm in Buckland. Between terms she began studying at the Byfield Academy with Mr. Joseph Emerson, a cousin of the famous Ralph Waldo Emerson. Still the ambitious young woman was not satisfied.

"Mr. Emerson," she announced to her tutor one afternoon, "I would like to learn chemistry and physics."

"Is there anything you don't want to learn?" Mr. Emerson inquired.

"I don't suppose there is," Mary admitted.

"Chemistry and physics are not given at the academies," Mr. Emerson told his eager pupil. "Those are college subjects."

"Then I shall have to go to college," Mary replied.

"That is quite out of the question and you know it," Joseph Emerson replied sternly.

"Don't worry, Mr. Emerson," Mary assured him with a smile, "I am going to college but only to engage a private tutor. Some one of these days, though, I hope to have a hand in establishing a college where young ladies will be welcome. Until then, we girls will just have to fight for our education."

The young woman marched off to Amherst where she was told that, of course, she could not be admitted to classes but that it would be possible for her to engage the Reverend Mr. Humphrey to give her private instruction in science. Mrs. Humphrey, Mary discovered, was a talented artist and the voracious scholar immediately signed up for lessons in drawing and painting as well.

By the time Mary Lyon had completed her courses with the Humphreys, she was one of the most accomplished young ladies in Massachusetts. She had, in addition, earned such a reputation as a teacher that some of the best girls' academies in New England were begging for her services.

"What I would really like to do," Mary confided to her brother and his wife, "is open my own school."

"Schools for young ladies are becoming so common these days," her brother replied, "that I fear we shall soon have our women better educated than our men."

"Not as long as the men can go on to places like Amherst and Harvard and Yale," Mary told him.

"I hope you're not suggesting that girls should be sent to college," her brother said.

"Don't look so shocked," Mary told him. "We women are a whole lot smarter than you think."

In 1821, when Mary Lyon was twenty-four years old, Emma Willard established a girls' school in Troy, New York, that rapidly became the talk of the country. Mrs. Willard was teaching her young ladies such unfeminine subjects as philosophy and higher mathematics. "At last," Mary Lyon declared, "someone is treating girls as if their brains are equal to boys'."

Although Mary herself had joined the faculty of Miss Grant's school in Ipswich, Massachusetts, she had never forgotten her dream of starting a college for girls.

"Of course, I wouldn't dare call it a college," she told Miss Grant. "Those are only for men. I think 'Female Seminary' would be a much more appropriate name."

"And will it be like Mrs. Willard's school?" Miss Grant wanted to know.

"Mrs. Willard has established a secondary school for girls," Mary said, "but I am planning to go a step farther. What I have in mind is actually a college, exactly like Harvard or Yale."

"It is a noble idea, Mary," Miss Grant said, "but you will need land and buildings and textbooks and a faculty. It sounds like an utterly impossible undertaking."

"One of my favorite mental exercises," Mary replied calmly, "is distinguishing between what is very difficult and what is utterly impossible." She took a deep breath. "This, I am quite sure, will only be very difficult."

Mary decided to launch a fund-raising campaign among the women of Ipswich. "We shall see how they react to my plan," she said. Putting on her best bonnet and her nicest smile, Mary Lyon sallied forth to begin her life's work. It meant rapping on every door in town.

"Good afternoon, Mrs. Atwood," Mary would say, "I'd like to talk to you about a project that is very dear to my heart."

The reactions of the good ladies of Ipswich were as varied as their wardrobes. At some homes, there was complete enthusiasm, at others outright hostility.

"A splendid idea," Mrs. Atwood might say, "I have always favored education for women—the more, the better."

On the other hand, Mrs. Atwood's neighbor, Mrs. Reynolds might raise her eyebrows and abruptly set down her teacup. "I have never heard of anything so unfeminine and anti-Christian in my life," she would declare and Mary Lyon would presently find herself being ushered to the door.

No matter how often she was rebuffed, however, Mary continued her afternoon calls. In a few months' time, her persistence was rewarded. Contributions to her projected Female Seminary totalled nearly a thousand dollars.

"At last I am on my way," she told Miss Grant.

Resigning her teaching position, Mary began traveling all over Massachusetts and Connecticut, begging for more funds for the new school. "Don't think any gift too small," she would tell people. "I want the twenties and the fifties, but the dollars and the half dollars, with prayer, go a long way."

Sometimes a poor woman selling eggs would slip a few

pennies into her hand, sometimes the wife of a prosperous attorney would ask her husband to write out a check for several hundred dollars.

"I promise you, you will not regret it," Mary told them. "Better education for girls will make better teachers, better homemakers and better women."

Bumping along the turnpikes in the high, uncomfortable stagecoaches, Mary Lyon soon became familiar with most of the regular travelers between Boston and New Haven. "And when will your seminary be ready to open?" a Connecticut merchant inquired during one of their journeys together.

"I am happy to say," Mary replied, "that the cornerstone will be laid on October 3rd."

"An historic occasion," the man replied. "I don't suppose any of you have met this lady," he went on, turning to the other occupants of the coach, "but mark my words, she is going to be famous some one of these days."

"Famous or infamous," snorted an elderly gentleman in the far corner of the carriage.

"I have no desire to be either," Mary replied. "I wish only to be known as a good teacher."

Mary had selected South Hadley, Massachusetts, as the site for her school. It was a small town in the valley of the Connecticut River only a few miles from her childhood home in Buckland. The institution was to be called Mount Holyoke Female Seminary.

Mount Holyoke's first president often recalled that bright October day in 1836 when the cornerstone was finally set in place. "A truly wonderful day," she exclaimed. "I have lived to see the time when a body of gentlemen have ventured to lay the cornerstone of an edifice which will cost about fifteen thousand dollars—and for an institution for women!"

The first building was to be four stories high. It would accommodate eighty pupils. By the time it was completed, Mary Lyon had had a hand in every step of the work. She consulted with the joiner about the woodwork, inquired after the mason's handling of his trowel, advised the painter on how to mix his colors. She inspected the floor boards, tested the windows, checked the hinges and tried all the door knobs. "I think," she declared at last, "that it will be a very sturdy edifice."

It was not until more than a year after the laying of the cornerstone, on November 8, 1837 that Mount Holyoke Female Seminary finally opened its doors to its first students. They came from all over New England and from four other states besides. There were, in all, one hundred.

Mary Lyon stood at the top of the grey stone steps watching them pour into the driveway. Some came in stagecoaches, others in fine carriages and still others in the plainest of farm wagons with their books and clothing wrapped in brown paper and tied up with string.

"Welcome to Mount Holyoke," Mary Lyon said as she greeted each one. "I hope you will be very happy here."

Trunks and parcels were quickly unloaded and the new students put straight to work.

"We're not quite settled yet," Mary explained. "If you'll

just lend a hand with this desk—and after that, you can help that gentleman over there who is tacking down the carpet. He's one of our trustees."

Even after the flurry of those first days, both students and teachers continued to take care of all the household tasks. "It is excellent training for future homemakers," Mary Lyon told her girls, "and besides, it will enable us to run the seminary on a stricter budget."

Louisa May Torrey, who later became the mother of President William Howard Taft, wrote home to her parents, "My work at present is moulding bread. I mould about ten loaves a day."

While many people praised the idea of domestic training, others found it a perfect excuse to condemn the new institution. Once when Mary went to visit a wealthy gentleman whom she had hoped would give a generous donation to Mount Holyoke, the man turned to his daughters with a sneer and said, "How would you like to go to a school where you were made to work in the kitchen?" The girls giggled and shook their heads emphatically. There was no further discussion and, of course, no donation.

Housework, though, was only an incidental part of the Mount Holyoke curriculum. The girls also studied mathematics, English, science, philosophy, political economy, modern languages and history, and at the end of each semester, they were expected to pass rigorous examinations. "You cannot imagine how trying they are," poet

Emily Dickinson wrote home, "because if we cannot go thru with them all in a specified time we are sent home. I never would endure the suspense which I endured during those three days again for all the treasures of the world."

Many of the parents inquired about singing and drawing, two subjects which had always been considered essential for refined young ladies to know. "Of course, we shall include them," Mary Lyon assured them, "but to study such ornamental branches without a good basic education would be like polishing cork or sponge instead of marble."

The girls at Mount Holyoke quickly adjusted to the arduous schedule which their headmistress had set for them. Besides their long hours of formal instruction each day, they were also required to participate in daily calisthenics classes as well as religious exercises. At night, by the light of their whale oil lamps, there was more studying and pages and pages of written assignments, all this on top of their household tasks. One young woman reported, "I rise at half past three in the morning, for my chum and myself make the early fires, eleven in the domestic hall and two in the dining hall."

On Thanksgiving Day, though, there was a special treat. "We had the privilege of sleeping as long as we wished in the morning," a grateful student wrote home to her mother, "provided we were ready for breakfast at eight o'clock."

Despite its strict rules and high standards of deportment and scholarship, young ladies from all over the Eastern seaboard were eagerly clamoring for admission to Mount Holyoke. Enrollment quickly swelled to 250 and another 250 girls had to be turned away for want of space.

Even as a busy school principal, however, Mary Lyon never forgot those cherished moments of her own girlhood when she had taken time from her chores to romp in the fields with her brothers and sisters or to sit by herself at the top of her favorite hill.

"Never be reluctant," she told her students, "to take a few hours out of each week simply to relax and enjoy yourselves."

The energetic schoolgirls needed no urging and the grueling hours of study were often interrupted for sleigh rides and picnics and leisurely walks through the nearby woods.

In the twelve years that Mary Lyon served as principal of Mount Holyoke, nearly two thousand girl were graduated from the school. Many became missionaries, many more, teachers, and more than a few married and settled down to raise families. As Miss Lyon had so confidently predicted, their fine education gave them a more intelligent and mature outlook on life and enabled them to find happiness in whatever way of life they chose for themselves.

Fittingly, the school which had been Mary Lyon's life became, in a way, the cause of her death. When one of the girls died during an epidemic of fever at Mount Holyoke, Mary, although she, too, was ill, insisted on gathering all of the young ladies together to comfort them on the loss of their fellow student and to exhort them to lead even more exemplary lives themselves. The following day, the fifty-two-year-old principal was confined to her bed with a raging fever and two weeks later, she was dead.

Today, her beloved Female Seminary is finally called a college, having been officially incorporated in 1888. She herself is enshrined in the Hall of Fame at New York University, her statue inscribed with a quotation from her last talk to her students. The words are an admirable statement of Mary Lyon's life and character: "There is nothing in the universe that I fear, but that I shall not know all my duty or fail to do it."

THREE

ᕙ Elizabeth Palmer Peabody

If a certain dentist in Salem, Massachusetts, had been able to earn a decent living for his family, America might have lost one of its most important educators.

As it was, the dentist, Dr. Nathaniel Peabody, had the misfortune to be practicing at a time when few people gave any thought to their teeth except to have them yanked out when they started to ache, and his wife and daughters were forced to teach school in order to balance the family budget. It was one of these daughters, Elizabeth Palmer Peabody, who started the first American kindergarten.

Despite what she called her "life of proud poverty," Elizabeth Peabody was descended from two of New England's most distinguished families and she and her sisters were often invited to tea at the finest homes in Salem.

"Why can't we live in a house like this?" Sophia Peabody

would murmur as she stared enviously at the intricate Aubusson rugs and gleaming mahogany furniture.

"Perhaps we will some day," Mary would whisper cheerfully.

"I wouldn't count on it," Elizabeth would tell them both on the way home. "The best thing we can do is get a good education and learn to support ourselves. Personally, I'd much rather do that than just be an elegant lady sitting around all day drinking tea out of Staffordshire cups!"

Occasionally the three sisters would be invited to a ball which they usually declined with regrets.

"I'm afraid we cannot afford to keep three young ladies in ball gowns and satin slippers and white kid gloves," Mrs. Peabody would sigh.

Her decree was seldom accepted without a few tears from Mary and Sophia but Elizabeth was usually much too busy reading Shakespeare to waste time brooding over anything as trivial as a party.

Mrs. Peabody had taught at the academy in North Andover before her marriage and when three young sons appeared to put an even greater strain on the family finances, she took up her parlor carpet and established her own school right there in the house.

That meant that the Peabody ladies had no place in which to receive guests or to be "at home" in the afternoons, but Mrs. Peabody swallowed her pride and went to call on her more prosperous neighbors.

"Wouldn't you like to send Martha—or Anne—or Serena —to my new school?" she would ask.

Although Mary and Sophia Peabody often played dolls and wandered through the woods gathering violets, poor Lizzie had scarcely any childhood at all. Her mother's classes were so popular that she was quickly pressed into service as an assistant and by the time she was sixteen, she was forced to put on a sober dress and a solemn face and become Miss Peabody to the pupils in the little parlor school.

If Elizabeth Peabody minded growing up so fast, she never mentioned it to anyone. Instead, she seemed to enjoy her work as a teacher. In whatever free time she had left at the end of the school day, she studied Latin with her father who had once taught at Phillips Andover Academy. When she had mastered Virgil and Horace, she next determined to learn Greek.

"It seems to me," Elizabeth Peabody announced to her mother one day, "that Mary and Sophia are old enough to take over my work in the classroom. I would like to go to Boston."

It was 1822 and Elizabeth Peabody was only eighteen years of age, but although many families would have been horrified at such a suggestion Dr. Peabody and his wife had always encouraged their daughters to be independent. "By all means, go, Lizzie," Nathaniel Peabody told his oldest daughter. "Perhaps you can even find someone to teach you Greek while you're there."

Lizzie laughed, but no sooner had she arrived in Boston and found herself a few pupils to help pay her room and board than she began to inquire after someone to give her

Greek lessons. The tutor she finally discovered was a nineteen-year-old clergyman. She called him Waldo but his full name was Ralph Waldo Emerson.

Before she even started her lessons, Lizzie had mastered half the textbook and when she had finished, Emerson refused to accept any fee for his work.

"You knew Greek before we even started," he protested to his gifted student. "It would be dishonest of me to accept any money for teaching you."

Boston had whetted Elizabeth Peabody's appetite for further travel and when she was offered a position as a governess for a family in Maine, she quickly accepted. Standing there on the deck of the Kennebec steam packet, however, Elizabeth Peabody could not help wondering if she would be happy in her new job. She need not have worried. Her new employer, Dr. Benjamin Vaughan, boasted a library of 10,000 books at a time when Harvard College had very few more and Lizzie Peabody had never been known to be unhappy around books.

On her very first morning in the Vaughan household, the new governess tiptoed downstairs before breakfast to peek at the impressive array of leather-bound volumes that lined the walls of almost every room.

"I see you are interested in my library."

The deep masculine voice almost made Elizabeth drop the copy of *Hamlet* she held in her hand.

"Oh, Dr. Vaughan," she said, breathing a sigh of relief as she turned to confront the master of the house, "you startled me."

"I'm so sorry, Miss Peabody," Benjamin Vaughan said. "I didn't expect to find you up so early."

"I can't help being fascinated by this wonderful library," Elizabeth explained nervously. "I just love books."

"So do I," said Benjamin Vaughan, returning her smile. "And you will make me very happy if you will use my library whenever you please."

Lizzie Peabody was overjoyed. She now had a chance to perfect her French by reading Voltaire and she could also dip into the plays of Sophocles and Euripides or the speeches of Cicero. During her stay with the Vaughans she read everything she could lay her hands on including a complete volume on the laws of the state of Maine.

There were a number of other young people living near the Vaughan's estate and they soon formed a weekly reading and discussion group. After attending one meeting Elizabeth Peabody began wondering for the first time in her life if she had not been spending too much time at her books. A number of nice looking young men belonged to the group and Lizzie found herself desperately wishing they would pay some attention to her.

"Mary and Sophia are always telling me to fix up my hair and wear prettier clothes," Elizabeth Peabody mused. "They said I could be a real beauty if I would only make the effort."

Hurling open the door of her wardrobe, Lizzie plowed through her dowdy governess clothes until she found the Sunday dress she had brought with her from Boston and never worn. It was black with wide crimson bands around the sleeves and hem and when Elizabeth Peabody studied herself in the looking glass, she was pleased with the girl she saw there.

"Now I must remember to be pleasant and agreeable," she told herself as she sallied forth to the next meeting of the reading club. "I must make these young men think of me as a pretty girl—not a school teacher with a head full of Latin and Greek and literature and history."

Lizzie's efforts to make herself attractive were so successful that the gentlemen were all vying for her attention that evening. One of them, in fact, was so entranced that he began calling on her regularly. For awhile Elizabeth almost fancied herself in love with him, but when the young man proposed marriage she had to say no.

"I'm afraid I am not ready to get married," she told him gently. "Not now, surely, and perhaps never. There are just too many things I want to do before I settle down to keeping house."

When Mary Peabody heard about the proposal her sister had refused, she nodded understandingly. "Lizzie," she told her older sister, "you are already in love with two things—learning and teaching. I don't think you will ever find a man who will interest you as much as they do."

Mary herself eventually married educator Horace Mann and Sophia became Mrs. Nathaniel Hawthorne but Elizabeth remained devoted to her one and only love—education.

Soon after her return from Maine she started a country day school in Brookline only a few miles outside of Boston.

Miss Peabody quickly became the darling of all her students. Besides concentrating on their spelling and penmanship, she also took pains to correct them for any faults of character that came to her attention. The class tomboy was brought to task for being "unfeminine," and a young lady with blonde ringlets was exhorted lest she become vain. Sometimes Elizabeth wondered if she was being too hard on the youngsters but they did not seem to mind and, indeed, showered her with bunches of wildflowers, gifts of rosy apples, and secret notes thanking her for her kindness to them.

Unfortunately, Elizabeth Peabody paid so much attention to her pupils and so little to her account books that she was eventually forced to close the Brookline school.

The invincible Miss Peabody refused to be discouraged, however. She would use her new found leisure to turn out a series of history books.

"I've been wanting to write them for ages," she told her publisher. "This seems like the opportune moment."

Ever since the day when she had first donned grown-up clothes and gone to work in her mother's school, Elizabeth Peabody had been helping to support her parents and younger brothers. Even now she could not relax. When her history books did not make as much money as she had anticipated, she took to the lecture platform.

"Shocking!" gasped the prim matrons of Massachusetts.

"Who ever heard of a lady standing up and making a speech in public?" they clucked disapprovingly.

No one had heard of it, of course, but that didn't stop Elizabeth Peabody. She talked about history and social problems to women's meetings all over the state and even the ladies who had been scandalized by her boldness came to hear her.

"Very interesting," they conceded and Miss Peabody was soon deluged with offers to speak.

Much as she enjoyed her experiences on the lecture circuit, Elizabeth still longed to return to the classroom, and when she discovered that Bronson Alcott was planning to open a school, she immediately volunteered to work as his assistant.

So impressed was Alcott with this brilliant young woman that he lost no time in accepting her offer and later even named one of his daughters after her. This same girl was portrayed by another Alcott daughter, Louisa May, in her famous book, *Little Women*. It is amusing to think that quiet gentle Beth was actually the namesake of another Elizabeth who was anything but shy.

When Bronson Alcott's Temple School collapsed after a storm of protest from outraged parents who objected to his unusual teaching methods, Elizabeth Peabody found herself once more in straitened circumstances.

Undaunted, she decided to open a bookshop. "But not an ordinary bookshop," she told her friends. "This will be a place where people who are interested in literature can meet and talk about some of the books they are reading."

The citizens of Boston had never heard of a lady

shopkeeper before and they were even more surprised to discover that she was stocking works in French and German. "Miss Peabody's foreign bookshop," they began to call the place.

"Let them call it whatever they please," said Elizabeth airily. "I'm sure we shall not want for customers."

Sure enough, some of the most interesting people in New England made the shop at 13 West Street their headquarters—Ralph Waldo Emerson, Henry Thoreau, Margaret Fuller and James Russell Lowell. Encouraged by her friends, Elizabeth also installed a printing press in the back room and became a publisher. One of her first offerings was a pamphlet denouncing slavery. She also published Nathaniel Hawthorne's *Twice Told Tales* as well as *The Dial,* a magazine of poetry and essays written by a group of New England thinkers who called themselves Transcendentalists.

Exciting as these literary ventures were, they were unfortunately not very profitable.

"I'm afraid I just have no head for business," she complained to her old friend Ralph Waldo Emerson.

Plagued as she so often seemed to be by failure, no one could have been more surprised than Miss Peabody herself when, at the age of fifty-six, she embarked on a new interest which proved to be the most sucecssful one she had ever tackled. It was to make her reputation as an educator.

Somewhere in the vast array of books she was constantly

poking her nose into, Elizabeth Peabody had come across the writings of a German schoolteacher named Frederick Froebel.

Froebel advanced the rather revolutionary theory that young children should be happy in school instead of miserable, and he outlined a plan for organizing special classes for five- and six-year-olds which he called *kindergartens*, or "children's gardens."

Elizabeth Peabody would not rest until she had learned everything there was to know about Froebel. She discovered that he himself had had a most unhappy childhood and he was therefore determined to bring joy into the lives of other boys and girls.

"Let the little ones have some exercise," was one of Froebel's first decrees. "It is not good to make them sit up straight as soldiers all the time."

Froebel was also anxious to give young children an appreciation of music and rhythm, a love of color and form, and an interest in the world of nature outside the classroom.

"Above all," said Froebel, "let us make school a pleasant place—not a prison."

"This man is wonderful," Elizabeth Peabody told her sister Mary. "I could not agree with him more."

Now Elizabeth Peabody would not stop until she had convinced America that there should be a "children's garden" in every school in the country. It was not an easy job. Even raising funds to start a model kindergarten of her own required a great deal of effort.

The irrepressible Miss Peabody, however, was more than up to the task. Whenever she could, she visited teachers' colleges and schools to discuss the project and she was constantly making the rounds of her wealthier friends to beg for their support.

Once she visited the home of a friend in Newport, Rhode Island, arriving without so much as an overnight bag.

"But Elizabeth," exclaimed her hostess, "where are your things?"

"My toothbrush is in my pocket and I'm wearing my nightgown under my dress," Elizabeth told her. "But let's not waste a minute. I want to tell you all about Frederick Froebel and his wonderful kindergartens."

By 1861, Elizabeth Peabody had raised enough money to open America's first English-speaking kindergarten at her home on Pinckney Street in Boston. (Mrs. Carl Schurz, whose husband was a distinguished figure in American politics, had established a German-speaking one in Wisconsin a few years earlier.) One of Elizabeth's first students was Maud Howe, the daughter of her Newport hostess.

The new school was an immediate success but still Elizabeth Peabody was not satisfied. "I will not be happy until I have gone to Germany to see the original Froebel kindergartens," she declared.

The Peabody finances were in their usual unsettled state but Elizabeth's many friends rushed to her assistance. "Send Miss Peabody to Germany" became the rallying cry and contributions soon came pouring in from all over the eastern seaboard.

"Eleven hundred dollars!" exclaimed Elizabeth when the money was finally totalled up. "I never realized so many people cared."

Elizabeth made the most of her trip to Europe. She visited museums and churches and art galleries and castles, but nothing, she found, gave her quite as much pleasure as visiting the German kindergartens.

She studied the equipment carefully—the brightly colored pegs, the wooden blocks, the paints and the clay. It must all be copied for use in American classrooms. She also visited several of the schools where kindergarten teachers were trained.

Eventually, however, Elizabeth Peabody began to grow restless. "I can hardly wait to get home and start campaigning for more American kindergartens," she told one of her German friends.

No sooner had Elizabeth Peabody stepped off the boat than the lecture circuit began. North, south, east and west, wherever she could find a group of people who were willing to listen, Elizabeth Peabody would talk about kindergartens. Once at a luncheon, she became so engrossed in the topic that she talked on and on without stopping until she was finally interrupted by the maid who asked if she might reset the table for dinner.

Spurred on by Miss Peabody's enthusiasm, kindergartens were opened in St. Louis and New York, and Kate Douglas Wiggin, author of *Rebecca of Sunnybrook Farm*, started one in San Francisco.

"We must have trained teachers," Elizabeth would also remind her supporters.

She herself had persuaded two of Froebel's disciples to open a school for teacher training in Boston and she never ceased recruiting students for them. Whenever she saw a young girl who seemed a likely prospect she would march right up to her and say, "Have you ever considered teaching kindergarten, my dear?"

It was amazing how many new teachers she discovered in this way.

One of Miss Peabody's earliest recruits was a young lady named Lucy Wheelock who later founded a famous Boston school for teachers.

It was Lucy Wheelock whom Mary Peabody Mann asked to accompany her older sister to New York in 1878 when Elizabeth insisted on attending a meeting of the Froebel Union which she had been instrumental in founding.

"Elizabeth," her sister Mary told her bluntly, "you are well past seventy, your eyesight is failing and you have already had one stroke. There is no reason in the world why this meeting cannot proceed without you."

"Poppycock," snapped Elizabeth and since there was no arguing with this formidable lady, Lucy Wheelock was dispatched to keep an eye on her.

"Above all," Mary Mann warned, "don't let her out by herself."

But the very first morning, Elizabeth Peabody arose at dawn and sneaked out of the hotel room while Lucy was still asleep. When the young woman discovered what had happened, she was frantic with worry, but at 8 A.M. Miss Peabody sailed blithely into the room and announced that everything was in order for the meeting.

"The lectern is in just the right place and the chairs are all set up," she said. "Of course, I had to wake up the janitor to let me into the hall. I hope he didn't mind too much."

"But Miss Peabody," Lucy protested, "you shouldn't have gone over there alone. I was worried sick about you."

"My dear child," Elizabeth told her sternly, "I am quite old enough to take care of myself."

Elizabeth Peabody's life spanned almost the entire nineteenth century—from 1804 to 1894. In the course of those ninety years, she had known almost every influential writer and thinker in the country and she had been active in any number of worthy causes, from the abolition of slavery to the fight for women's suffrage.

When she died, however, her friends chose to honor her with a memorial to the cause she had loved best. They established the Elizabeth Peabody House, dedicated to the promotion of kindergarten education—a fitting tribute for a little girl who grew up too soon.

FOUR

ᴄ∕(*Alice Freeman Palmer*

In 1902 an American lady died in France. The nurse who had been tending her in her last hours spoke no English and knew nothing about her patient, yet she turned to the bereaved husband with tears in her eyes and murmured softly in French, "Monsieur, she was truly a remarkable woman."

Just how remarkable a woman she had been caring for, the nurse probably never knew, but a few years later when George Herbert Palmer published a biography of his wife, he was deluged with letters from all over the country. Statesmen and schoolgirls, millionaires and outcasts, clerks and country wives all wrote to add their praises to the story of a wonderful lady named Alice Freeman Palmer.

The list of Alice Palmer's accomplishments is not a long one. President of Wellesley College for six years and Dean of Women at the University of Chicago for three, her greatest triumph was her unique ability to bring happiness into the lives of everyone she met.

Alice Freeman was born on a farm near Colesville, New York, in 1855. A real country girl, she loved the grass and the trees, the horses and the cows. On spring afternoons she would roam through the fields and flop lazily down to dabble her fingers in the cool brook that snaked across their meadowland.

Farm life was not always so carefree, however. More often, Alice Freeman was busy gathering eggs in the barn, helping with the planting, tending to the housework or minding her younger brother and sisters. The Freemans had few books or newspapers to read and barely enough food to eat. "There was never any meat on the table," Alice recalled, "and a keg of salt mackerel was a special treat."

It sometimes seemed as if life could get no grimmer, but then Alice's father, James Warren Freeman, decided to become a doctor. "I think it will make things a little bit easier for us," he told his wife, "but you and the children will have to manage by yourselves while I am studying."

"We will manage," his wife resolved bravely. It meant more work and less food for everyone but the family struggled through until James Freeman had completed his studies at Albany Medical School.

"It was a bad time," his oldest daughter remembered, "but it taught us the value of sacrificing our present comforts for important goals."

Dr. Freeman moved his wife and four children to the

village of Windsor and although country doctors have never been noted for their enormous incomes, the family was able to live a lot more comfortably than they had on the farm.

Windsor boasted its own academy which Alice attended until she was seventeen years old. By then she had formed some very definite opinions on what she wanted to do next.

"I've decided to go to college," she told her mother and father.

"College!" said Dr. Freeman, sitting bolt upright in his rocking chair. "Where on earth did you get that idea?"

"I've been thinking about it for quite awhile," Alice replied calmly.

"But there are no colleges around here," Dr. Freeman protested.

"Then I shall have to go where there are some," said Alice.

"Do you realize how much it will cost?" her father demanded. "It seems to me that if anyone goes to college in this family, it should be your brother Fred."

But Alice Freeman stood firm. "Father," she vowed, "I am going to get a college degree even if it takes me until I am fifty years old. If you will pay my way now, I promise to see Fred through school when it is his turn and both my sisters, too, if need be."

Dr. Freeman could see that he was licked. "All right," he cried, throwing up his hands, "you win. You can go to college—although I can't imagine where."

"I've been thinking about the University of Michigan,"

said Alice. "It's a very good school and they've just started admitting women students."

That September, James Freeman accompanied his daughter out to Ann Arbor and sat in on her interview with the President of the University. "I am very much impressed with your daughter," President Angell told him. "Even though her preparation has not been as thorough as we usually require, I am going to admit her for six weeks on trial."

The minute Alice Freeman kissed her father good-bye, she was off to the library to begin working. Besides her regular classes in history, Greek, and English literature, there were make-up courses in Latin and mathematics, but when her six weeks' trial was over she had more than proved that she could do the work. In fact, at the end of the first semester, one young man in her class told his parents, "There's a girl in my class who knows everything. *Everything!*"

Alice Freeman received her degree from the University of Michigan in 1876 and after that she entered into a phase of her life which she later referred to as "the years of drudgery."

Dr. Freeman's already tiny income had dwindled to a new low and he was obliged to remind Alice of her promise to help in educating her younger brother. "I have no intention of going back on my word," she assured him, but it meant that she would have to settle for the very first job she was offered. It turned out to be a position teaching Greek and Latin at a girls' seminary in Wisconsin.

A short time later, both her sisters developed tuberculosis and she decided to resettle the entire family in Saginaw, Michigan, where she had accepted a post as principal of the local high school—a singular honor for one so young and a woman besides. With the burden of so many family responsibilities on her frail young shoulders, Alice Freeman paid little attention to the news that a man named Henry Fowle Durant was opening a girls' college in Wellesley, Massachusetts, about fifteen miles west of Boston. She was somewhat startled, therefore, when she received a note from Durant inviting her to join the faculty of his new school as an instructor in Greek.

For an instant, Alice's imagination soared. How marvelous to be a part of a women's college at a time when there were only a handful in the entire country. What an exciting chance to mould the minds of growing girls and introduce them to a whole new world of ideas. But it was out of the question.

"I am sorry," she wrote to Henry Durant, "but family obligations prevent me from accepting your generous offer."

Still determined to capture Alice Freeman for his faculty, Henry Fowle Durant simply waited a few months and then posted another letter. "How about an instructorship in mathematics?" he asked this time.

Once again the answer had to be no and Henry Durant might have given up entirely had not his old friend Professor Angell of the University of Michigan chanced to see his former student in action in the classroom. He saw

her teaching high school English and listened in amazement as teenaged boys discussed novels and plays and lyric
poetry as enthusiastically as if they were talking about
hunting or fishing.

A letter went speeding off to Henry Durant in Wellesley, Massachusetts. "You simply *must* have her," Angell
wrote.

When Durant's third invitation arrived, Alice Freeman
did not dare refuse it. Most of her family obligations had
been fulfilled, the rest could be managed by sending home
part of her salary each month.

"This is a very exciting experience for me," she confessed as she hugged her family good-bye. "I don't know
when I've been so happy."

Alice Freeman had been asked to head the history department at Wellesley but the minute he met her, Henry
Fowle Durant began hatching even greater plans for the
twenty-four-year-old high school principal from Michigan. "See that little dark-eyed girl," he said to one of the
school's trustees, "she will be the next president of Wellesley."

During those early years when the college was still quite
young, there was a great deal of work to be done arrang-
ing dormitories and classrooms, planning courses of study
and assembling competent professors. Alice Freeman was
soon working so hard that Wellesley almost lost its future
president. Having inherited the family tendency toward
tuberculosis, Alice, who had never been particularly

strong anyway, collapsed with a hemorrhage of the lung. "Six months to live," was the doctor's grim prognosis.

Depressed and frightened, Alice almost wished she could die right there on the spot. "I haven't had a chance to do half the things I want to do with my life," she thought sadly, "and now there is no more time."

The next morning when she awoke there was sunshine flitting across her room and a pair of birds were chirping a happy duet outside. "I am not going to lie here waiting to die," said Alice Freeman, regaining some of her old spirit. "I am going to find myself another doctor."

The following week, she took off for New York to consult the famous specialist, Dr. Willard Parker. "Is it true that I have only six months to live?" she asked.

Dr. Parker examined her thoroughly and inquired about all her symptoms. "If you have character and courage, you can live," he told her finally. "Get plenty of fresh air and rest and eat wholesome food. I think you have many good years ahead of you."

Alice Freeman returned to Wellesley and faithfully followed Dr. Parker's advice. She was never troubled with tuberculosis again and when she was examined several years later, the doctors discovered that the lesion on her lung had completely disappeared.

When Wellesley's founder, Henry Fowle Durant, died in 1881, Alice Freeman, the youngest teacher on the entire faculty, was asked to become president of the college. "But we can only give you three hours to think it over," the trustees told her. Hitching up her horse and carriage, Alice drove out to the countryside where she could ponder in peace the momentous decision that lay before her.

As she looked around at the rolling hills and green farms, she was reminded of the scenes of her girlhood. Things had been so uncomplicated then. But as she sat there contemplating the view, she also remembered lugging the heavy pails of water in from the well, scrubbing the big kitchen floor, washing and dressing her brother and sisters and walking with them to school. Alice smiled to herself. "I guess nothing in life is completely perfect," she sighed, "but you have to keep on going just the same."

There were endless worries and responsibilities in the new office but Alice Freeman's chief problem was her age. At twenty-six, she was only a few years older than the girls she was expected to take charge of. "What wouldn't I give for a few grey hairs," she murmured.

The first thing she decided to do was to call a meeting of the senior class. "As some of you may know," she told them, "I have been asked to take over President Durant's post. It is a difficult task and I can only manage if you will help me."

"But what can we do?" one of the girls inquired.

"If you will maintain discipline among yourselves," said Alice Freeman, "it will leave me free to carry on my administrative duties."

Since the new president had elected to treat her students like mature women, they quickly began to act that way.

Not only did they keep order in their own ranks, they also saw to it that the other classes behaved as well.

Strict as she was about educational standards, Alice Freeman was also anxious to make all of her students feel at home at Wellesley. For some time she lived in one of the dormitories and even after she moved to her own cottage, she dined with the girls each day and was always available to discuss their problems.

She knew the name of every student in the school and always took a deep personal interest in each of them. Years later, she could attend alumnae meetings in various parts of the country and greet former graduates as warmly as if she had seen them only the day before. "Why Helen Townsend," she would say, "do you still like to read English novels? And how is your old roommate, Grace Rogers?"

Alice Freeman set rigid standards for herself and she expected her students to do the same. "Whatever we have to do, we can always do," she used to say. Again, when a girl complained about a particularly difficult schedule, she would tell her, "It is hard, but I know you can do it."

"Knowing that she thought I could do it made me determined to succeed," the girl said afterward.

In order to get the most out of her four years at Wellesley, Alice Freeman realized that a girl must be adequately prepared to enter college. She remembered well her own difficulties during her first weeks at the University of Michigan and she had often seen other young women laboring under similar handicaps. To eliminate this problem she started a secondary school, Dana Hall, right near Wellesley, and others staffed by her graduates were later organized in other parts of the country.

Although Alice Freeman could be very strict when the occasion demanded it, she was not without a sense of humor. Once during a lengthy argumentative faculty meeting at the college, she was called out to talk to the housekeeper from Dana Hall. "The girls want you to come over and see the dress rehearsal of a French comedy they are putting on," she was told. "I have a carriage waiting outside."

"Wait just one minute," Alice whispered with a twinkle in her eye.

Returning to the meeting, she announced soberly that she had been called away for a few moments on urgent business. Then she slipped off to the rehearsal where she sat in the front row, laughing uproariously during the entire show. When she returned a half hour later, the opposing factions at the meeting had all made peace and their business was concluded in a matter of minutes.

In her efforts to make Wellesley an outstanding school, Alice Freeman frequently called upon distinguished faculty members from nearby universities to give courses at the college. One man, a handsome professor of English from Harvard named George Herbert Palmer, took a great interest in the attractive and clever young president. When he chanced to meet her again in Cambridge at the home of a mutual friend, George Palmer lost no time in getting better acquainted and the pair became engaged on Alice's thirty-second birthday, February 21, 1887.

Although she had promised to keep their troth a secret for awhile, Alice could not resist wearing her sparkling new engagement ring in public and the halls of Wellesley were soon buzzing with the news. "She is forsaking her career for love," many people said disapprovingly. In those days, a woman had to be dedicated either to her work or her husband. She could not have both.

Alice Freeman refused to be dismayed by her critics. She had given eight years of her life to Wellesley and developed it into the kind of school that Henry Fowle Durant had dreamed it would become. Someone else could now handle the job just as well as she. The trustees begged her to remain as long as possible and she agreed, staying in her office until nearly midnight on the very night before her wedding.

Instead of curtailing her interest in education after her marriage, the new Mrs. Palmer was able to do even more in the field. She remained on Wellesley's Board of Trustees and also served on the Massachusetts State Board of Education where she worked for better normal schools, free high schools and qualifying examinations for teachers.

She also took to the speaker's platform to lecture on behalf of girls' colleges. Her audiences, who generally thought of educated women as a homely, rather opinionated bunch, were charmed by her good looks and delightful personality and usually went away determined to send their daughters to Wellesley so they would turn out like that lovely Mrs. Palmer.

Busy as she was, Alice Palmer never ceased to be a loving and devoted wife. Once when her husband was sick in a Boston hospital, she noticed that the pillow he was using was extremely uncomfortable. While he was asleep, she left the room, walked four miles back to their house in Cambridge and returned with a softer one for him. Another time, when she herself had to undergo minor surgery, George Palmer was busy working on an important paper. Loathe to disturb him, she went off to the hospital alone and when the operation was all over, sent him a message telling him where she was.

In 1892, Alice Freeman Palmer was asked to become Dean of Women at the newly founded University of Chicago and her husband was offered the chair of history. The couple agreed that Dr. Palmer was too deeply rooted at Harvard to be happy anywhere else but Alice herself was persuaded to accept the deanship with the proviso that she would not have to stay in Chicago more than three months of the year.

One of Alice Freeman Palmer's lifelong interests was the education of underprivileged children. Determined to bring at least a little joy into their drab lives, she would volunteer each summer to work in the vacation schools operated in the Boston slums.

"Tell us how to be happy," one of her pupils once asked her. "Commit something good to memory each day," Alice

Palmer told them. "Look for something pretty and do something for somebody else."

The following week, the youngsters reported on how well they had kept the three rules. One little girl found a beautiful sight in "a sparrow taking a bath in the gutter and he had on a black necktie and was handsome." The same child, left all alone at home to mind her baby brother, was feeling bad because she couldn't go out and play with her friends. "Then I saw the baby's hair," she said. "A little bit of sun came in the window and I saw his hair and I'll never be lonesome any more."

Years later when George Herbert Palmer published his wife's biography, a young lawyer read the book and showed it to his wife. "My goodness," said the woman, "I was that poor little girl, and I remember that teacher so well. I never knew her name but we always called her 'the beautiful lady.' She opened up a whole new world for me of poetry and music and lovely ideas."

If she had known this, Alice Palmer would have considered her work worthwhile, for once when someone had urged her to write a book about education, she had scoffed at the idea. "I am trying to make girls wiser and happier," she had said. "Books don't help much toward that. They are entertaining enough but really dead things. Why should I make more of them? It is people that count. You want to put yourself into people; they touch other people, these, others still, and so you go on working forever."

While on a tour of Europe with her husband, Alice Palmer was stricken with an unusual ailment of the stomach that required immediate surgery. It was a dangerous operation and the doctors held out little hope of recovery. Alice herself was perfectly aware of her condition and the night before the operation, she handed Dr. Palmer a long list of her engagements for the months ahead. "You must write to all of these people," she told him, "so they will not be disappointed."

A few days later, Alice Palmer died peacefully in a hospital in France. She was truly, as her nurse said later, a remarkable woman, and perhaps her husband, George Herbert Palmer, best explained why. "Each eye that saw her blessed her," he wrote. "Each ear that heard her was made glad."

FIVE
Mary McLeod Bethune

Samuel and Patsy McLeod lived in a sagging pineboard cottage on the outskirts of Mayesville, South Carolina. A wooden tub of water on the back porch was their kitchen sink, and bacon for dinner was considered a feast, but Sam and Patsy McLeod never dreamed of complaining. Grateful for the Emancipation Proclamation of 1863 which had given them their freedom, they considered themselves lucky to have their own small cotton farm, luckier still to be able to keep their children and not have them carted away to be auctioned off on a slave block.

Their daughter Mary, who was born in 1875, was not so easily satisfied. White folks, she noticed, lived in better houses and had plenty to eat. Was it just because they were white? Or was it also because they knew how to read and write and could get far better jobs than uneducated Negroes?

"I want to go to school," Mary McLeod told her father

one day as they trudged home after a hard day's work in the cotton fields.

Samuel McLeod shook his head sadly. "There are no schools for colored children," he said.

Mary's reaction was a mixture of rage and resignation. Why should colored children be treated any differently from white children? one part of her demanded angrily; but another part of her meekly conceded that education was just one of many things no Southern Negro could ever hope to have.

"That's when I started praying," Mary McLeod remembered much later.

Mary always believed that it was her prayers that sent Miss Emma Wilson to Mayesville. What else could explain the teacher's sudden appearance at the McLeods' cabin asking if there were any young ones who could be spared from the fields long enough to get an education?

Instinctively, the whole family turned to Mary, the brightest and most ambitious of them all. "We can spare this one," Samuel McLeod said, pushing his daughter forward.

"You mean you're going to teach me to read?" the wide-eyed child asked breathlessly.

"That's right," Miss Wilson assured her, "and I wouldn't be at all surprised if you turn out to be a very good student."

"Oh yes, Ma'am," Mary stammered. "I mean . . . I'll do my best." In her heart she was breathing a quiet thank you to God for answering her prayers.

Going to Miss Wilson's school not only meant that Mary would be the first of the McLeods to know how to write her own name, she would also be the first to own a pair of shoes. Great heavy brogans they were, with metal tips to keep them from wearing out too fast. They could not have been very comfortable for a girl who was used to scampering about the fields in her bare feet, but blisters and bunions were a small price to pay for the opportunity to get an education.

Young Mary McLeod never missed a day at the rickety one-room schoolhouse which Miss Wilson had grandly christened the Mayesville Institute, but as graduation time drew closer, the once eager student began to neglect her studies.

"I'm surprised at you, Mary," Miss Wilson said to her one day. "Have you grown bored with school?"

"Bored?" exclaimed Mary in astonishment. "How could anyone ever get bored with learning things?"

Miss Wilson laughed and put her arm around the slender schoolgirl. "What are you planning to do after graduation?" she asked.

Suddenly tears welled in the soft brown eyes. "That's just the trouble," Mary sobbed, "there doesn't seem to be anything to do except go back to picking cotton."

For awhile it seemed that Mary's fears were quite justified. She received her diploma from the Mayesville Institute and the whole family turned out to applaud but after that, it was back to the same weather-beaten shanty and the rows and rows of cotton.

"Lord, help me to go to school some more," Mary prayed but this time it seemed like the Lord was too busy to listen to a little colored girl's prayers.

Then, one day, a familiar figure appeared at the cabin door.

"Miss Wilson," Mary cried, running to embrace her former teacher.

"I've brought good news for you, Mary," Miss Wilson told her. "A dressmaker named Mary Crissman from Denver, Colorado, has decided to use her life's savings to provide an education for a Negro child . . . and you deserve it more than anyone else I can think of."

The Mission Board of the Presbyterian Church, which had sent Miss Wilson to Mayesville, also ran a school for girls called Scotia Seminary in Concord, North Carolina. Miss Crissman's gift would pay for Mary McLeod's tuition there.

Scotia Seminary was full of surprises for the bewildered cotton farmer's daughter. Inside the front entrance, there were two wide staircases. Taking a deep breath, Mary clung desperately to the banister, not daring to confess that she had never before in her life climbed a flight of stairs. At dinner that evening she saw her very first table-cloth and stared curiously at the knife and fork that were set beside her plate. It took several days' practice before she learned how to use them.

The most important new thing that Mary McLeod discovered at Scotia, however, was that there were white people who paid no attention to the color of a person's skin.

men and women whose only concern was to turn ignorant children into intelligent and useful citizens.

The school curriculum included algebra, Latin, English composition and history. Mary also joined the debating team and the choir and discovered something she had never known before. One afternoon while strolling through the town of Concord, she passed the Cannon textile mills and heard the heavy looms thumping away inside, weaving endless bolts of cloth to be made into sheets and towels.

"So that's what happens to all that cotton I used to pick!" Mary exclaimed.

Though her days in the fields were over, Mary McLeod was by no means finished with hard work. During her seven years at Scotia, she spent every summer vacation working as a maid to earn enough to buy books and clothing for the next school year.

By the time she was ready to graduate, Mary had made up her mind to go to Africa as a missionary.

"Why don't you apply to the Moody Bible Institute in Chicago for training?" Scotia's director, Dr. Satterfield, suggested. "I will get in touch with the Presbyterian Mission Board and inquire about the possibility of a scholarship."

A few weeks later, two replies came whizzing back through the mails. Yes, Mary McLeod would be accepted as a student at the Moody Bible Institute. Yes, there would be a scholarship to cover her tuition, provided once more through the generosity of Miss Mary Crissman.

"Thank you, God," murmured the aspiring missionary.

The little girl who had once thought it a great adventure to trek five miles down the road to school was now going to journey all the way to Chicago. Moreover, her work at the Bible Institute would give her even greater opportunities to travel. The school operated its own Gospel Car, a railroad coach that took students into poverty-ridden sections of the country to establish mission churches and Sunday schools.

Once during a tour of the Dakotas, the itinerant preachers stayed overnight at the home of a minister whose five-year-old daughter had never before seen a Negro.

"Mother," the child cried when she saw Mary McLeod, "that lady didn't wash her face and hands. She's all dirty."

Mortified, the mother glanced apologetically at their guest.

Mary smiled. "That's perfectly all right," she told the girl's parents. Then lifting the child up on her lap, she brushed the tiny hand along her cheek. "See," Mary said, "the color doesn't come off. It stays exactly the way God made it."

The little girl was soon completely entranced with the gentle lady who had come to visit in her parents' house. "Look at this vase of flowers," said Mary, pointing to the centerpiece in the middle of the dining room table, "God made them many different colors, just as He did with people. When they are gathered together, they make a beautiful bouquet."

The little girl nodded and hugged her new friend. As

she climbed down from the comfortable lap, the child's mother took Mary McLeod's hand. "If the only thing you accomplish on this journey is to give my child that lesson," she said, with tears in her eyes, "your trip will have been worthwhile."

Mary McLeod had no sooner completed her course at the Bible Institute than she hastened to apply for a missionary's post in Africa.

"I'm sorry," the director of the Mission Board told her, "there are no openings right now. Perhaps if you could wait a few years. . . ."

All the studying and the work and the prayers had been for nothing! Mary had to struggle to hold back the tears. "Yes . . ." she whispered numbly. "Thank you . . ."

Even when Dr. Satterfield told her about an opening for a teacher at a school in Augusta, Georgia, Mary could not muster any enthusiasm for the job.

"I suppose I might as well take it," she told him half-heartedly. "It doesn't really matter what I do now."

Mary McLeod's blues seemed to evaporate, however, the minute she arrived at the Haines Normal Institute and met Miss Lucy Laney. Born in slavery, Miss Laney's owner had taught her to read and write and encouraged her to browse through his library. After the Civil War, Miss Laney set out to share her knowledge with every Negro youngster she could lay her hands on. Her determination infected Mary McLeod at once. "I began to realize," she said, "that Africans in America need Christ and school just as much as Negroes in Africa." The disappointed missionary had found a new dream—she would dedicate her life to the education of her people.

Not even Albertus Bethune, the handsome young tenor from the church choir, could dissuade her. "I am a teacher," she warned him, "and I intend to remain one." Albertus Bethune came calling anyway. Before long, the two young people were married and a year later their only son, Albert McLeod Bethune, was born.

Having a child of her own only made the new mother more anxious to go on with her teaching. Every time she looked down at the sleepy little baby in her arms, she realized how few opportunities the world would hold for him—unless someone like herself created them. "The only answer is a decent school," she decided, "and I will have to get busy and start one."

When young Albert was five years old, construction began on the Florida East Coast Railroad. Most of the laborers were Negroes who would work for a fraction of the pay that white men demanded. They lived in the squalid shanty towns which had sprung up all along the line and their children played in the garbage littered gutters that ran between the wretched cabins.

"I can't believe things are that bad," Mary Bethune said when a friend told her about the situation. "I shall have to see for myself."

With Albert by the hand, she set off for Daytona Beach, took one look at the raggedy, underfed youngsters in Colored Town and made up her mind. "This is where I'm going to start my school," she said.

Unbelievable as it may seem, the founder of what was to become the Daytona Education and Industrial Training School for Negro Girls had only a dollar and a half to her name. Undaunted, she persuaded a good-natured landlord to let her borrow a cottage he owned on Oak Street. "You shall have the rent just as soon as I can scrape it together," she promised him.

Junk yards and public dumps were combed for useable furniture, boxes and upside-down baskets doubled as chairs, ink was distilled from boiled elderberries and charred pieces of wood became pencils. On October 3, 1904, Mary McLeod Bethune finally opened her school. "And this is only the beginning," she vowed.

In less than two years, the enrollment at Mary Bethune's school had swelled from six to 250 pupils and the energetic principal was frantically searching Daytona's Colored Town for a larger piece of property on which to erect a new building. When she finally discovered a suitable plot, she called on the owner to inquire about the price.

"What on earth do you want to buy that for?" he said scornfully. "It's swampy and buzzing with mosquitoes and everyone in the neighborhood dumps their garbage there."

"Really?" said Mrs. Bethune. "I never even noticed. All I could see was a place where boys and girls could learn to face life with their hearts full of faith, hope and love."

The stunned landowner agreed to let her have the plot

for two hundred dollars. "Five dollars down," he told her, "and the rest within two years."

It took a great deal of begging and borrowing before Mary Bethune managed to scrape together the five dollars but she finally presented it to the man—a collection of dimes and pennies and quarters all tied together in a clean white handkerchief. The garbage dump was hers and she was determined to make it a showplace.

Concerts by the school choir were turned into fund-raising events and once a week the principal herself would set off on her bicycle to knock on every door in Daytona. Her simple direct manner usually made friends for her at once.

Millionaire soap merchant James N. Gamble started her off with $150 and his subsequent gifts added up to many times that amount. Another good friend was wealthy sewing machine manufacturer Thomas H. White who, at his death, left the school a trust fund of $67,000.

In two years, a four story building opened on the site of the former garbage dump. Above the front entrance were the words "Enter to Learn," and inside over the same door, "Depart to Serve." Ten years later the Daytona Educational and Industrial School had over 400 students and was offering a full high school course as well as training in home economics, teaching and nursing.

With the help of some of her students, Mary McLeod Bethune decided to embark upon still another project. In the forests of northern Florida, Negroes, working for low wages and all the rum they could drink, were hired to tap

the pine trees that yield the gummy sap from which turpentine is distilled. The workers lived in makeshift villages
called turpentine camps where conditions were so miserable that drunkenness, tuberculosis and malnutrition were
run-of-the-mill afflictions.

Mary McLeod Bethune set out to rehabilitate the resi-
dents of one camp and within five years she had established
a chain of mission schools all over the northern part of the
state. Under her watchful eye, camp children learned how
to read and write and their parents were taught the fun-
damental rules of cleanliness as well as how to prepare
wholesome meals and budget their meager wages.

Another of Mrs. Bethune's projects was the establishment of McLeod Hospital. In 1911 one of her students developed a case of acute appendicitis and the distraught
teacher hurried to the local hospital for assistance.

"No niggers allowed," an attendant informed her rudely.

"But this is an emergency," Mrs. Bethune protested.

"So what?" snarled the attendant.

Spying a white-coated doctor in the hospital corridor,
Mary Bethune rushed over and explained her problem. The
sympathetic physician agreed to perform the operation
but afterwards, hospital authorities left the girl to recuper-
ate on a back porch just behind the kitchen.

"I was so angry even my toes clenched with rage," Mary
Bethune recalled later.

Back at her school, Mrs. Bethune fired out a furious barrage of letters to all her friends and benefactors, and succeeded in raising $5000 to erect what eventually grew into

a twenty-bed hospital staffed by both white and Negro doctors assisted by her own student nurses. In more than one emergency the white citizens of Daytona sought help at McLeod Hospital and its warm-hearted founder saw to it that no one was ever turned away.

In 1923, the Daytona Educational and Industrial School merged with a nearby institution for men and became the coeducational Bethune-Cookman College. By then, its director was already winning recognition as one of the country's outstanding educators.

Once, as president of the National Association of Colored Women, she addressed a huge meeting in Los Angeles on the need for more scholarships for Negro girls. Beaming proudly beside her on the dais sat an elderly white lady. At the end of her speech, when Mrs. Bethune was presented with a huge bouquet of roses, she promptly offered them to the woman at her side.

"This," she said introducing her friend to the audience, "is Miss Mary Crissman who donated the scholarships which provided me with my own education."

The long road from the cotton fields of South Carolina eventually stretched to Washington, D. C. In 1930 President Herbert Hoover invited Mrs. Bethune to participate in the White House Conference on Child Health and Protection. His successor, Franklin D. Roosevelt, relied even more heavily on her services. First appointing her to tackle the employment problems of Negro young people, he later asked her to administer an Office of Minority Affairs of the National Youth Administration.

Mary Bethune hesitated at first. "I have to look after my college," she said.

"But, Mary," one of her friends pointed out, "do you realize that this is the first such post created for a Negro woman in the United States?"

There was no longer any question about the matter and President Roosevelt was delighted to receive her acceptance.

"Mrs. Bethune is a great woman," he said. "I believe in her because she has her feet on the ground; not only on the ground but deep down in the plowed soil."

In spite of all her accomplishments, Mary Bethune was still keenly aware that many people considered her a second class citizen. Often denied admittance to hotels and restaurants and pushed into separate waiting rooms in railroad terminals, Mary Bethune nevertheless liked to remember a more gratifying incident which occurred during a luncheon at the White House.

"Several southern ladies were there and knowing how they felt about Negroes, I tried to make myself as inconspicuous as possible," she said.

Suddenly, Mrs. James Roosevelt, the President's mother, caught sight of the guest, took her by the arm and steered her straight to a chair at the right of Eleanor Roosevelt.

"It was the place of honor," Mrs. Bethune wrote later. "I can remember how the faces of the Negro servants lit up with pride when they saw me seated at the center of that imposing gathering of women leaders from all over the United States."

Another time, during World War II, she was sitting in the white people's section of the Atlanta airport. When a policeman came over and asked her to move, a young soldier came to her rescue.

"Let this woman alone," he snapped. "This is the sort of thing we are fighting for."

Mrs. Bethune served as Assistant Director of the Women's Army Corps during the war and afterwards was a consultant on interracial understanding at the San Francisco Conference which drew up the charter for the United Nations.

Most precious of all her honors and awards, however, was the Spingarn Medal which Mary McLeod Bethune received from the National Association for the Advancement of Colored People. The medal is given "for the highest or noblest achievement by an American Negro during the preceding year or years" and in winning it, Mary Bethune joined such other distinguished members of her race as scientist George Washington Carver, singer Marian Anderson, labor leader A. Phillip Randolph and UN peacemaker Dr. Ralph Bunche.

In 1950, at the age of seventy-five, Mary McLeod Bethune made a sentimental journey back to Mayesville, South Carolina. The cotton fields were still there and so was Miss Wilson's school, even more rickety than ever and still, after more than sixty years, the only school for colored children in the area.

"There is so much more to be done," sighed Mary

Bethune, "but I am growing too old. Someone else will have to do it."

Mary McLeod Bethune died in 1955, but the school which she founded continues to grow in importance and influence, vigorously carrying forward the work to which she devoted her life.

SIX

Alice Morrison Nash

Pretty, bright-eyed Alice Morrison had wanted to be a teacher for as long as anyone in the town of Northwood, New Hampshire, could remember. She talked about it and dreamed about it and when it came time to graduate from Northwood High School, she finally did something about it. She enrolled at the Literary and Bible School, only a few miles away at New Hampton, for a two-year course in teacher training.

Not until the spring of 1900, just a few months before she would receive her diploma, did the enthusiastic young student teacher begin wondering just where she was going to teach. There were hundreds of elementary schools all over New Hampshire but Alice was anxious to see a new part of the country. Perhaps Boston . . . or New York . . . or even somewhere out west.

Then one morning a classmate stopped her in the corridor. "I have just heard of a job that might interest you," she said. "They are looking for a teacher at a school near Vineland, New Jersey. It is an institution for the feeble-minded."

"The feeble-minded?" Alice said. "But I don't know anything about working with children like that."

Her friend shrugged. "Neither does anyone else," she said.

Alice Morrison's first impulse was to dismiss the suggestion. It was going to be hard enough starting work as an inexperienced teacher without getting involved with youngsters who were already a problem. Besides, she had never even heard of Vineland, New Jersey. The more she thought about it, however, the more interesting it sounded. Alice Morrison had always said she liked challenges. Here was her chance to prove it.

The next morning she grabbed her classmate by the arm. "What is the name of that place in New Jersey?" she demanded, "and to whom do I write to ask about the job?"

A few weeks later, the newly graduated teacher was on her way to the sleepy south Jersey town of Vineland. As she settled back against the green plush train seat and watched her New Hampshire hills slide away beside the silvery steel tracks, she began to wonder about the job that lay ahead of her.

Alice Morrison had never really known anyone who was mentally retarded but she had occasionally heard whispered tales of "idiots" and "feeble-minded children." Most people acted as if it were some sort of disgrace and a family unfortunate enough to have such a child rarely mentioned it in public.

The young teacher had made a special effort to find out something about The Training School. She discovered that it had been started thirteen years earlier by a Philadelphia minister named Stephen Olin Garrison in his own home at Millville, New Jersey. In 1888, Garrison acquired larger quarters in nearby Vineland and the institution was moved to its present location. By the time Stephen Olin Garrison died, the school which he had started in a frame house with seven children had acquired at 170-acre campus, ten separate buildings and an enrollment of over 100. Garrison's leadership had passed to another dedicated man named Edward Ransom Johnstone.

"Professor Johnstone will be my first employer," Alice Morrison thought nervously as she climbed off the train at Vineland. "I hope he will be patient with his newest faculty member."

The instant she walked into the Superintendent's office Alice Morrison knew she had nothing to worry about. There sat Professor Johnstone in his big leather chair, a tiny blonde girl on one knee and three small boys at his side. He was telling them about the escapades of Brer Rabbit.

"Oh my goodness," the Professor said, looking up and seeing the young woman standing in the doorway. "You must be Miss Morrison."

He was about to shoo his spellbound audience away

but Alice Morrison protested. "Oh, please finish the story," she begged. "I am enjoying it just as much as the children."

She slipped quickly into a chair beside the desk and waited until Brer Rabbit had finally hippity-hopped back home from his latest adventure and the four delighted youngsters had dashed off to play. Then Professor Johnstone stood up and gave his new teacher a more formal welcome to The Training School.

"We are all pioneers here," he told her, "but I think there is a great deal of work that can be done with these children. Our job is to find out the best way to do it."

Having been trained at New Hampton only as an elementary school teacher, Alice Morrison was somewhat surprised to discover that her work at Vineland would go far beyond the classroom. She had no sooner unpacked when Miss Vernon, who supervised the teaching staff, knocked on her door.

"Miss Morrison," she said, "I would like you to take charge of one of our boys' dining rooms this evening."

Alice Morrison followed Miss Vernon obediently across the darkened grounds but when they arrived at the dining hall in Moore Cottage, she was dismayed to find, not the lively small boys she had anticipated, but twenty full grown men, many of them taller than she was.

The young woman stood at the door too startled to even take her place, but Miss Vernon, sensing her reaction at once, turned to a slim, rather stoop-shouldered "boy."

"Tim," she said, "would you please ask the blessing to-night?"

"Why sure, Miss Vernon," Tim said cheerfully. Then while everyone bowed their heads, he said, "Dear Lord, we thank you for the good food we are going to eat tonight and for all the good things you have given us today."

Alice Morrison joined the chorus of Amen's and quickly took her place at the head of the table. Soon Tim was introducing her to his other schoolmates and telling her all sorts of stories about them.

"I like you, Miss Morrison," he said when the meal was over. "You can be Timmy's friend."

"I'd love to be your friend," Alice Morrison told him. "Perhaps you will be in one of my classes."

When she spoke to Professor Johnstone about it, however, he told her quite bluntly, "Tim's mind is simply not capable of absorbing classroom knowledge. He has already begun his life's work as an errand boy here at the school."

Twenty-year-old Alice Morrison was aghast. "But surely he could learn to read," she said, "and perhaps even to do simple arithmetic."

"You must remember, my dear," Professor Johnstone warned her, "working with the mentally retarded is not quite the same as dealing with regular students. Maybe experience will be your best teacher though. I'll assign Tim to one of your classes."

Alice Morrison never forgot the hours she toiled with her new student. She would put a simple word on the board such as CAT, spell it for him and have him spell it back. The next day when she would ask Tim to spell CAT he would laugh and say, "Oh, I love cats. Did you see the new kittens over at the feed-house?"

With numbers it was not much better. Miss Morrison would put 2 and 2 on the board, add it up for him and then ask Tim to try it. He would go up to the front of the room and say, "That's a two and that's a two."

"And how much are both of them?"

Tim would laugh and shrug his shoulders. "What do you want to know that for? There's the two two's right there."

Slowly and painfully, Alice Morrison was learning her first lesson about working with the mentally retarded. She had to accept their grimly limited abilities.

One warm spring afternoon as she was strolling across the school grounds brooding over her failure to make a student out of Tim, Alice Morrison encountered Professor Johnstone. He seemed to sense at once what was troubling her.

"You mustn't let Tim discourage you," he said. "No one believes in education more than I do. But I also believe there is more to life than reading and writing. In spite of his poor mind, Tim is one of our most cheerful and energetic pupils here at the school. I can't think of anyone who better proves that saying of mine which I like to think of as our motto—happiness first, then all else follows."

Alice nodded. Professor Johnstone was right, she knew, but she still found it hard not to be discouraged. It was not just Tim who left her baffled and confused. None of her classes seemed to be going as well as she had hoped.

Just then Alice Morrison heard someone calling her name. It was Tim hurrying along on one of his errands. With a bright smile and a happy good morning, he suddenly popped a piece of paper out of his pocket. "I have a letter for you, Miss Morrison," he announced.

The paper was a mass of scribbling. "Maybe you'd better read it to me, Tim," Alice Morrison said.

"Sure," Tim replied and then, staring at the paper he began to recite a message he had obviously been memorizing for some time: "Miss Morrison is very pretty. Timmy likes her a lot. She is the best teacher in the world. She teaches Timmy how to spell CAT and add two and two. And now that he's learned so much, maybe she should let him graduate."

Suddenly Alice Morrison realized that Professor Johnstone was right. She had no business trying to change Tim. He was a completely delightful person. All he needed was love and the freedom to be himself.

"Tim," she said, "from now on, no more lessons for you. This will be your graduation day."

Tim skipped gleefully off on his errand and Alice Morrison went on her way feeling better than she had in months. "And from now on," she promised herself, "Professor Johnstone's motto will be my motto, too. Happiness first, then all else follows."

This need for love and security among the mentally

retarded had been uppermost in the Reverend Garrison's mind when he started The Training School. He wanted to create a separate village where his boys and girls would live in their own cottages with house mothers and fathers to care for them. "The Cottage Plan," as it is called, is still used at Vineland and has been copied in similar schools throughout the world.

Alice Morrison never ceased to be amazed at the family spirit which developed so naturally through the plan. Once when a cold felled both the house parents at one cottage, their youngest charge, a small boy named Johnny, returned from his classes to discover a new man in charge.

"Where is Pop?" Johnny wanted to know.

The man explained that both Pop and Mom, as the children called them, were ill. The doctor was taking care of them and they would be back on duty just as soon as they were feeling better.

Johnny listened gravely and then, with tears in his eyes he knelt down on the floor and began to pray. "Dear God," he whispered anxiously, "please make Pop and Mom well. They are awful sick and we need them—specially me."

With patience and understanding, Alice Morrison was soon making more progress with her retarded classes than she had ever dreamed possible. Those who could learned reading and writing and basic arithmetic. Some of the girls were taught to cook and do housework and many of them became quite expert. The boys had a chance to help out on the school's own farm. A few of the young people did so well that they received salaries for their services at the school and, in turn, paid for their own room and board.

Not all of Vineland's children, however, were so self-sufficient. There were some who had to be taught to dress and feed themselves and many more, often well into their teens, who would never progress beyond the kindergarten level in their work. Others suffered from defective speech, hearing or sight.

In those days, The Training School at Vineland was one of the few places in the country where any effort was being made to cope with the problems of the mentally defective. "We have learned so much working day by day with these youngsters," Alice Morrison once remarked to Professor Johnstone, "I wish there was some way we could use our knowledge to train other teachers in the same field."

"I have been thinking the very same thing," Professor Johnstone replied. "In fact, I was going to ask you to draw up a series of courses that we might incorporate into a summer session for special teachers."

By the summer of 1904, Alice Morrison had organized the Vineland Summer School for the Training of Teachers of Backward or Mentally Defective Children. The first class consisted of five students who paid $25 for their lodging and tuition and were given six weeks study in the general field of retarded children as well as courses in teaching methods, training and discipline.

Alice Morrison's old friend Tim always looked forward to the opening of these summer sessions. He was invariably on hand to help the visiting teachers find their rooms, give them a tour of the grounds or simply make them feel at home just as he had done for his friend Miss Morrison on her first evening at Vineland. The summer students were soon calling him "dear old Tim" and many who returned for a second session after a lapse of several years were amazed when Tim greeted them by name and rushed to help them with their suitcases.

One day, Professor Johnstone was seated beneath a beautiful chestnut tree in the center of the campus giving a very serious lecture to one of his summer classes. As he neared the climax he began to raise his voice and make emphatic gestures with his hands. Just at that moment, Tim rounded the corner of the administration building, saw the Professor apparently giving a group of visiting teachers a good scolding and shouted, "That's right, 'Fessor, give it to them! That's just what they need!"

The class broke into uproarious laughter and Professor Johnstone said sternly, "Tim, you old rascal, what do you mean by upsetting my lecture like this?" Tim looked crestfallen but as soon as he realized that the Professor was smiling at him he rushed over and said, "I didn't mean to do anything bad, 'Fessor, really. I only wanted to help you."

"I am certain," Alice Morrison said later, "that those teachers learned more about working with retarded children in that moment than they did from many a book on the subject."

Until courses of this type were finally taken over by the universities, Vineland's summer session was the only school in the country for teachers of special classes. It lasted for twenty-seven years under Alice Morrison's direction and its enrollment totalled over 900 men and women from public and private institutions all over the world.

Alice Morrison's years at Vineland were not devoted exclusively to her work, however. A few months after her arrival, she made friends with a tall dark-haired young man named Charles Emerson Nash. Ted, as his friends called him, had been born on a farm near Albany, New York, and had earned his way through teachers' college by singing and playing in bands and orchestras.

The Reverend Garrison had advertised for a male teacher for his new institution in the very same paper where Ted had inserted a notice for a job. The minister and the young man got together and Ted soon found himself bound for Vineland, New Jersey, as a teacher of band music, military drill and gymnastics.

Alice Morrison seldom saw her fellow instructor without at least one child by his side. Often when he appeared, a whole tribe of boys and girls would be swarming after him. She noticed that he never failed to wait for the youngest and slowest of them to catch up to him and take his hand.

"Mr. Nash," she told him one day, "next to Dr. Johnstone, you seem to be our most popular faculty member."

"Oh, I never have any trouble getting along with kids," Ted Nash replied with a grin, "but I wish I could get some of the teachers to pay a little more attention to me."

"But they do pay attention to you," Alice Morrison protested quite seriously.

"Not all of them," Ted Nash said. "Why there's one

very attractive young lady who hardly speaks to me. You know her—that one from New Hampshire. I think her name is Morrison."

Alice Morrison started to laugh. "Why, Mr. Nash," she said, "you know that isn't true. I always talk to you. Why I'm talking to you right this minute."

"Yes," Ted admitted ruefully, "but most of the time you only talk to me about teaching or The Training School or the schedule for the summer sessions. Couldn't we ever talk about you . . . or me . . . or us?"

Alice Morrison found herself blushing. "I . . . suppose . . . we could," she stammered.

"Good," Ted Nash said. "How about Sunday afternoon? I know a marvelous spot for a picnic."

Before long, the two teachers were spending all of their Sunday afternoons together and few people at the school were surprised when they announced their engagement several months later. They were married in Professor Johnstone's parlor on January 27th, 1909. "And," said the Professor after the ceremony, "I hope you'll settle right here in Vineland and live happily ever after."

Alice and Ted Nash had no intention of settling anywhere else. The former band instructor became one of the most respected and beloved members of The Training School faculty and eventually took over Edward Ransom Johnstone's post as superintendent of the institution, a post which he held until his death in 1953.

Alice Nash was appointed Director of Education at the

school in 1925; she also served as editor of *The Bulletin,* a publication which is sent to experts in the field of mental deficiency in twenty-nine countries. In 1952, Mrs. Nash was named Educational Consultant at The Training School.

During the more than fifty years that Ted and Alice Nash spent at Vineland, they witnessed some important milestones in the history of special education. One of the Reverend Garrison's original plans for his school had been the establishment of a center for the study of scientific and medical data on retarded children. Although Garrison never lived to fulfill his dream, his successor, Professor Johnstone, created just such a laboratory in 1906. Its director was a psychologist named Dr. Henry H. Goddard.

It was Goddard who brought back from Europe the Binet-Simon Tests of Intellectual Capacity, one of the first tests designed to measure human intelligence. Using these as a yardstick, Goddard was able to classify retarded youngsters according to their capabilities. From his experience with the children at Vineland, Henry Goddard devised the intelligence tests that were used by the United States Army in World War I—the first time in history that an entire army was organized on the basis of brainpower. These same tests were later adapted for use in education and industry.

While scientists have made some significant discoveries about the nature of mental retardation, its causes and cure remain a mystery. Heredity, once thought to be a major factor, now seems to be but a small part of the picture. Far more cases seem to be caused by infections, birth injuries or some type of prenatal damage. Recent investigations point to German measles, mumps and other viruses striking the mother during pregnancy.

Although progress has been slow, the research continues. "We always hoped for experts who could find some way of making these children normal people again," Ted Nash once said. "We're still always hoping and our laboratory never ceases trying."

Meanwhile, the faculty at The Training School goes on coping with the everyday problems of children who never grow up. In spite of improved methods and tested educational techniques, the best formula still seems to be the one that Professor Johnstone and Alice and Ted Nash discovered many years ago—love.

"You'd be surprised how it pays off," says Alice Nash. "Under treatment here, lots of youngsters go home cured. I know it's hard to believe, but at least 100 boys who were at one time or another pupils here, passed their draft board examinations and went into the service in World War II. One of them even became a marine."

Not all of Vineland's students have progressed so astonishingly, of course. Most still move in the shadowy world that so tragically separates them from their normal brothers and sisters. Thanks to the efforts of devoted teachers like Alice Morrison Nash, however, their world of shadows is surprisingly bright. It has become a world of sunshine and innocent laughter, a world where happiness comes first, then all else follows.

SEVEN
Ella Flagg Young

In 1910, Ella Flagg Young was probably the best known teacher in the United States. In addition to being Chicago's first and only woman superintendent of schools, she had also been elected first woman president of the National Education Association, the nation's largest organization of members of the teaching profession. Strangely enough, however, Ella Young herself had never even graduated from high school and, in fact, did not even learn to write until she was ten years old.

Ella Flagg was born in Buffalo, New York, in 1845. She was a frail child and her mother, convinced that Ella would never live to lead a normal life, refused to enroll her in school. "It would be much too strenuous for such a delicate youngster," Mrs. Flagg declared.

For this reason, Ella's education was obtained in a highly unusual fashion. To give her plenty of fresh air and sunshine, her parents insisted that she take up gardening but when she was not busy in her flower and vegetable beds, Ella would often sit and watch her father in his forge. He was a skilled metal worker and his little daughter soon learned all about his craft and the various tools he used in it. In later years, she often used to say, "I had manual training before such things were thought of, especially for girls."

Although her parents owned an impressive library and her older brother and sister often brought books home from school, Ella showed little interest in learning to read until one day shortly after her eighth birthday. The morning paper arrived with screaming headlines announcing a fire in one of the Buffalo schools.

"Think of it," Ella's mother said, "little children no older than you burned to death or killed when they had to throw themselves out the windows!"

Ella, in tears, grabbed the paper and insisted that her mother read the whole story to her. As soon as she had finished, the girl demanded to hear it again. Then, still sobbing, Ella took the newspaper off to her room where she pored over every word of the disaster, trying to remember exactly how her mother had read it. By the end of the afternoon the fire itself was almost forgotten.

"Mother, Mother," cried the eight-year-old, bursting triumphantly out of her room. "I can read! I can read!"

After that there was no stopping the eager little girl. She pored through the Bible and read and re-read her father's books on history and philosophy. The flowers and vegetable gardens that were once so faithfully tended were soon neglected and would have been forgotten completely if she had not persuaded her brother Charles to take over their care.

"You do the planting and weeding," she told him, "and I'll pull over one of these nice big wicker chairs and read aloud to you while you work."

Ella's health had gradually been improving and by the time she was ten, her mother decided that she was well enough to be enrolled in the neighborhood grammar school. Her father had already trained her in mathematics and her extensive reading had taught her a great deal about history and geography.

"The one really new thing I shall learn," she said, "is how to write correctly."

The new pupil did indeed learn penmanship but she also learned another lesson which was to help her in her subsequent career. One morning her brother Charles had been particularly naughty and, as punishment, the principal had decided to spank him in front of the entire school. Ella could not bear to watch and she put her head down and began to weep. Suddenly Charles ran over and put his arms around his distraught sister. "Don't cry, El," he whispered. "I've got on three pairs of pants."

Ella Flagg never forgot the incident and although she later managed to laugh about it, she was always firmly opposed to any form of corporal punishment for the children in her charge.

When Ella was thirteen years old her family moved to Chicago. She had just graduated from eighth grade and was about to enter high school, but according to the rules in Chicago she must complete another year in their grammar schools before she would be eligible to go on to high school.

"But she has already done the work," Mrs. Flagg protested.

"I am sorry," the principal replied, "that it is the rule."

Although Ella was enrolled at the Brown School at the corner of Warren Avenue and Wood Street, she was bored from the very first day. She already knew all of her history and geography and she was far ahead of the class in reading and arithmetic.

"I sometimes think, Ella," her teacher sighed one day, "that you are wasting your time here with us."

"I think so, too," the thirteen-year-old replied and that afternoon she dropped her books in the front hall and announced to her parents, "I am not going back to school. I have already learned what they are teaching there."

After staying at home for two years reading and studying on her own, a friend persuaded Ella to take the examination for teachers in the Chicago public school system. She passed it with no difficulty but when the Superintendent of Schools looked over her application, he was appalled to discover that the would-be schoolmistress was only fifteen years old.

"Miss Flagg," he told her, "I cannot deny that you have done very well in the examination. You are well qualified to be a teacher in every respect except one—your age. Most girls of fifteen are still in school themselves."

Ella found it hard to suppress a smile, but she waited politely while the dismayed superintendent thought the whole situation over. Finally he said, "Would you like to attend one of our normal schools until you are old enough to begin work as a teacher?"

Ella accepted the man's offer and her experience at the normal school taught her another valuable lesson. As part of her courses in science, she was learning about the operation of a hydraulic press. Her father, who was watching her study, was annoyed to discover that instead of learning how the machine actually worked, she was simply committing its various parts to memory.

"She had a fairly good mind to start with," he complained to her mother, "but if she continues under such teaching, she won't have any mind left at all after awhile."

Ella realized that her father was absolutely right and although it meant spending several more hours on her assignment, she went over the explanation in her book very carefully until she completely understood how the press worked.

The following day, there was a picture of the hydraulic press on the examination with one important part left out. Ella, who knew how the machine operated, was the only one in the class to realize that the diagram was wrong. As a result, she was also the only one who did not fail the test.

"I decided then and there," she said, "that I would never let any students of mine memorize information without understanding it. My father was right. If someone with a good mind goes at his work that way, he will soon have no mind at all."

Before Ella had completed her second year at normal school, her mother began to have serious doubts about the career her daughter had chosen. "You have never been around young children," she said. "How do you know you will like them? And besides, you are so severe with yourself when you make a mistake, I'm afraid you might be just as stern with the little ones."

"I don't think you are right, Mother," Ella replied. "But there is only one way to find out."

The very next day, Ella asked for permission to visit a first grade class. She sat in the back of the room and watched the youngsters file in, the little girls with their pigtails and starched middy blouses, the boys with their baggy knickers and carefully slicked-down hair. She listened to them recite their multiplication tables and watched as they lisped their way through the beginning reader. She made friends with them in the schoolyard at recess and joined them in their games. By three o'clock that afternoon, Ella Flagg knew that she was not making a mistake. Teaching was the job she wanted.

"Children are the most wonderful creatures I have ever met," she told her mother. "I can hardly wait to have a class of my own."

Ella Flagg began her career at the Foster School and after eight months there, she was promoted to head assistant at the Brown School where she had been so bored only five years before. Unfortunately, her first years at work were marred by deep personal sorrows. Only two weeks after she started teaching her mother died and shortly after that, her brother Charles was killed in a railroad accident. In 1868 she married William Young, a close friend of her family's for many years. Her new husband died only a few months after their wedding and Ella had barely recovered from that shock when both her father and her sister succumbed to pneumonia.

In spite of the tragedy that seemed to be haunting her, Ella Young continued teaching. "I have lost all of my loved ones," she said. "From now on, the children of Chicago will be my adopted family."

A small woman with bright piercing eyes and simple tailored clothes, Ella Flagg Young was not just a doting mother to her large brood. More often, she was a stern father as well and her pupils quickly learned that she would tolerate no nonsense.

Once when she was serving as principal of the Skinner School a fist fight erupted in the schoolyard during lunch period. Ella Young handed the black and white shawl that she frequently wore to school to one of the teachers. "Put this on and go to the door," she said, "just to see what happens." The famous shawl had the same effect as a white flag waving in the midst of a battle. The scuffle ceased at once and there was no more fighting for the rest of the lunch hour.

No matter how strict she sometimes seemed with both the pupils and the teachers she supervised, Ella Young always had their best interests at heart. When she was a district supervisor, she noticed that the teacher in the fourth grade class seemed rundown. The next day, a bottle of iron tonic was delivered to her with a note from Ella Young. "Try some of this. I noticed how pale and peaked looking you seemed yesterday."

Another time, Mrs. Young visited a principal who was sick in the hospital. "And what will you do when you are discharged from here?" the supervisor demanded.

"I hadn't thought about it," the woman replied. "I guess I'll just take it easy around the house until I feel ready to go back to work."

"You'll do no such thing," Ella Young replied. "I am going to arrange for you to stay with some relatives in Florida. That nice sunshine will help you regain your strength to face our Chicago winters."

By the end of the week, the principal had received a train ticket to Florida along with strict instructions from Ella Young not to return until she was completely well again. On another occasion, when the sister of two of her teachers was seriously ill, Ella Young hired a trained nurse for the woman, paying her wages out of her own pocket.

Ella Flagg Young's outstanding work in the city's schools soon brought her to the attention of William Rainey Harper, the president of the University of Chicago. "I want you to become a professor in our education department," he told her.

"That's ridiculous," Ella Young said, "I have only studied two years at normal school. I can't be a professor without a college degree."

"It's the woman I want, not the degree," Harper replied.

Still Ella Young insisted that she could not accept the post, but Harper, determined to make her a member of his faculty, found a way to overcome her objections.

"We'll make you associate professorial lecturer in pedagogy," he said, "and the full professorship will be waiting for you whenever you feel qualified to accept it."

Inspired by William Rainey Harper's confidence in her ability, Ella Young not only joined the university faculty but also enrolled as a student as well.

"Now that you are finally a full-fledged college graduate," the president told her as he handed her her degree on graduation day, "I hope you will decide to accept my original offer of a professorship."

"I'd be delighted," Ella Young replied happily.

In 1909, Ella Flagg Young was appointed Superintendent of Schools for Chicago, the second largest educational system in the country. There are many stories of how she got the position. One version says that the Board of Education was interviewing prospective appointees one stifling June day. Anxious to get home, the board members listened wearily as one after another of the would-be superintendents discussed their qualifications for the job. Finally, Ella Flagg Young was ushered in. She sat down in front of them and started to talk and one by one, the drooping board members began to come to life. They had found their man—even though she happened to be a woman.

Although part of this story is undoubtedly true, the situation was actually a little more complicated. Chicago, then as it sometimes is now, was torn by a series of political feuds. There were a number of different factions on the Board of Education, each of which had its own particular candidate for the lucrative post of Superintendent of Schools. Since none of the group could muster a majority of votes, the board members finally decided to compromise by appointing the only applicant whose main interest was not politics, but schools. The plan was to hire Ella Young for a year while they worked out a way to get a man to take over.

If Mrs. Young was aware of what the Board of Education had in mind, she chose to ignore it.

"My only concern," she used to say, "is for the children of Chicago."

She was determined to make their school system the finest in the country. "One of the first things we must have," she told the Board of Education, "is a kindergarten in every school." More classrooms had to be provided, extra equipment ordered and specially trained teachers hired but before Ella Young was finished, every elementary school in Chicago had a kindergarten of its own.

Next on the list were manual training courses for the boys and domestic science classes for the girls. Equally important, Mrs. Young felt, was the addition of commercial subjects in the city's high schools.

"Not all of our young people will be able to go on for further training when they graduate," she said. "We must provide them with skills in bookkeeping and stenography so they will be able to earn a decent living."

Another of Ella Young's concerns was the health of Chicago's school children. She particularly worried about those who were frequently ill or who suffered from chronic diseases. "They need fresh air and sunshine just as much as reading and writing," she said.

At her suggestion, the Chicago schools started special fresh air classes which gave these youngsters a chance to be outdoors more often than their stronger schoolmates. Visiting the classes sometimes reminded Ella of her own frail childhood.

"I realize that these children need to be outdoors and that gardening is one of the most beneficial forms of recreation for them," she once told a friend with a smile, "but frankly, I spent so much time at it when I was a girl that I wouldn't care if I never saw a rake or a hoe or a patch of dirt again."

One subject which did interest Mrs. Young, though, was her adopted city. She instituted an elementary school course called Chicago in which the children learned all about the history and geography of the Windy City. The course included field trips to view the famous water tower that survived the terrible fire of 1871, strolls through Lincoln Park and visits to the Museum of Natural History.

Ella Young was as interested in her teachers as she was in their students. "Come in and see me," she often urged them and though there were 6000 members in Chicago's immense school system, she always found time for a visit with anyone who cared to take her up on her invitation. Sometimes, she would even invite a group of principals to her own home for tea and an afternoon of spirited conversation.

The teachers returned her affection. There were few who missed the lectures she gave each year at the opening of the school term. Said one woman, "These were the greatest inspiration I received from any superintendent during my long career."

Another confessed that she went mainly to enjoy the school superintendent's lively sense of humor. "That is one of the reasons we all flock to hear her," said the teacher, "and sit on the steps of the hall for an hour to be sure to get a seat."

Chicago's teachers knew that Ella Young was always on their side. She wanted them to have a voice in school organization and management and insisted that all of her suggestions be understood and endorsed by the teachers before they were adopted. "No one can work in another's harness," she used to say.

But when Ella Young proposed raising her teachers' salaries, the Board of Education drew the line.

"They are paid enough," growled one of the men. "We won't give them another cent."

His fellow board members grunted their agreement and Ella Flagg Young countered by submitting her resignation on the spot.

"I refuse to work for any school system whose policies I disagree with," she announced.

When the news of her resignation appeared in the morning papers, a group of irate Chicago citizens hurriedly called a mass meeting in protest. The huge auditorium was jammed with the school superintendent's devoted fans and one paper reported, "Chicago never before gave such a testimonial to any citizen as the meeting in behalf of Mrs. Ella Flagg Young."

By the time the meeting ended, the Board of Education was begging Ella Young to reconsider her action. Although Mrs. Young eventually returned to her job, the quarrel was by no means over. The Board of Eucation still had no intention of raising teachers' salaries. Once more Ella Young stormed out of her office and again the men, women and children of the city rallied to her support. The pay increases were finally authorized and Ella Flagg Young continued as Chicago's superintendent of schools until shortly after her seventieth birthday in 1915.

One of Ella Young's favorite quotations went like this:

> *I am only* one;
> *But, I* am *one.*
> *I cannot do everything*
> *But I* can *do* something.
> *What I* can *do, I* ought *to do;*
> *And what I* ought *to do,*
> *By the grace of* God,
> *I* will *do.*

Mrs. Young's life was an admirable summary of this principle. During the course of her long career in education, she was also a great friend of Jane Addams and an ardent supporter of the social work programs Miss Addams

introduced at Hull House. Ella Young was an equally enthusiastic agitator for women's suffrage. In fact, she herself was in the forefront of the fight for equal rights for
her sex when, in 1910, she became the first woman president of the National Education Association.

At that time, although women outnumbered men ten to
one in the teaching profession, the organization was con-
trolled completely by men, most of them college presidents and school superintendents. One group of classroom
teachers was determined to have a stronger voice in the affairs of the association. At the annual meeting in Ogdens-
burg, New York, they brushed aside the regular slate of
nominees and began campaigning for their own candidate
—Ella Flagg Young. When the ballots were finally counted,
Mrs. Young had been elected president of the National
Education Association by a vote of two to one.

At the outbreak of the First World War, Secretary of the
Treasury, William Gibbs McAdoo, asked Ella Flagg
Young to lend her talents to the Women's Liberty Loan
Committee. Though she was well over seventy by then,
Mrs. Young was delighted to accept the post. While trav-
eling about the country in the course of her work, how-
ever, she contracted influenza and died during the dreadful
epidemic of 1918.

In her memory, the women principals of Chicago set up
a special fund to be used for scholarships and medical care
for the city's needy youngsters. Even in death, Ella
Young had found a way to keep an eye on her beloved
children of Chicago.

EIGHT
⤳ Martha Berry

If you ever happen to be traveling through the piney mountains of northwestern Georgia, be sure to stop in and visit the Berry Schools. You will be amazed at the fine Gothic buildings, the sprawling 35,000 acres of woodland campus and the hundreds of eager students. You will be even more amazed to learn that in the beginning there was only an abandoned log cabin, three curious children and a remarkable lady named Martha Berry.

Martha Berry was born near Rome, Georgia, in 1866, the oldest of eleven children. Her father, Thomas Berry, was a prosperous cotton dealer and the family lived in a handsome house with stately white columns that was called Oak Hill.

Not everybody in Georgia, of course, lived in such fine style as the Berrys. As a young girl, Martha had gone to visit a friend whose family had a vacation home in the mountains. Exploring the forest trails, the two girls would often come to a rough clearing where some hill family lived in a ramshackle hut. Barefoot, half-naked children squatted by the cabin door staring sullenly at the strangers who had happened by. The women, dirty and unkempt, sweated over open fires cooking corn pone or hogback while their husbands, using crude tools and old-fashioned methods, struggled to earn a living from their wretched farms.

"Look at these poor people," Martha whispered to her friend, "see how thin and listless the children are."

The other girl nodded. "They never have enough to eat," she said, "and most of them don't even know how to read and write."

"Something should be done to help them," Martha replied.

Martha Berry went off to finishing school in Baltimore but returned when her father fell ill, to help him run his cotton business. Sometimes when the checks were all written out, the orders recorded and the books balanced, the young woman would wander off into the hills carrying gifts for the mountain children.

"You must learn to give wisely," Thomas Berry warned his daughter. "More than anything else, these people need a chance to help themselves."

One Sunday afternoon Martha Berry was sitting alone in the old log cabin playhouse at Oak Hill when she looked up and discovered three pairs of bright eyes peering at her through the open window.

Martha smiled and went over to talk to her uninvited

guests. They wore tattered overalls and ragged shirts and their bare feet were caked with dirt.

"Him and me's brothers," one of them spoke up, "from Trap Holler and our friend here is from Possum Trot.

"Do you go to school?" Martha wanted to know.

"Ain't got no school," the boy replied.

"And what about Sunday school?"

The boys looked surprised and Martha explained that Sunday school was a place where children learned about God and Jesus and the Bible.

"Oh, we'uns got a Bible," one of the boys volunteered, "only Pa cain't read it."

"Sit down," Martha invited them. "Let me tell you some of the wonderful stories that are in it."

The boys listened, wide-eyed, as she told them about Daniel in the Lion's Den, and David and Goliath, and the good Queen Esther.

"Can we'un's come back ag'in," one of them asked when she had finished.

"Of course," Martha replied. "Come again next Sunday and bring your brothers and sisters, too."

The following week, the little log cabin was jammed with children. First Martha showed them how to wash their hands and faces; then, when all the germs had been scrubbed away, she offered them cake and lemonade. She told them more about the Bible and she also taught them some hymns and talked to them about the trees and birds and butterflies.

"Be it all right ef Maw 'n Paw come next time?" one of the girls asked as she was leaving that afternoon.

"We'd be delighted to have them," Martha replied, little realizing that the grownups would respond as eagerly as their children. A week later, an enormous assortment of mountain families surged into Oak Hill. They came on mules and on foot, in oxcarts and sagging wagons, crowding into the little playhouse, ssh-ing the dogs and babies so as not to miss a single thing Miss Martha had to say. Poor Miss Martha could hardly concentrate on her stories that week. She was desperately trying to think of a better place to hold her Sunday meetings. She remembered an abandoned church she had seen over at Possum Trot about eight miles from Oak Hill.

"That will do very nicely," she decided.

The steps of the old building were sagging, and the rotting floor boards infested with fleas. On the very first Sunday a sudden cloudburst sent torrents of rain cascading down through the dilapidated roof. There was nothing to do but dismiss the gathering but Martha refused to let any of the highlanders leave until they had promised to repair the wretched building.

"It has to be done by next Sunday," she told them. "Who'll volunteer?"

There was a long silence before one of the men finally spoke up. "Miss Marthy," he said, "ef hit's a-rainin' this week, we cain't kivver hit, and if hit ain't rainin', we don' need hit kivvered."

Martha sighed. Could she really do anything with these mountain people, she wondered.

Nevertheless, she announced that there would be a working party the following Wednesday morning. She herself would provide meat and cakes. To Martha's surprise almost all of the men appeared and she put them to work at once with their hammers and saws. By sundown, the steps were sturdy, the floor boards patched and the leaky roof completely rainproof.

Martha Berry's horse and buggy were by now a familiar sight among the hill people. The children would run along beside her shouting, "Here comes the Sunday Lady," while their parents waved and called hello from their doorways.

The meetings at Possum Trot were going so well that Martha set about refurbishing two other neglected churches. That gave her three different sets of classes to supervise each week, but still it did not seem to be enough.

The children needed more than just songs and stories. "Show us how to write our names," a freckled-faced boy would demand. "How do you figger numbers?" his sister would ask shyly.

Before his death, Thomas Berry had given his oldest daughter a large tract of land. "It's the perfect place to build a one room schoolhouse," Martha said to herself. "Then my boys and girls can come every day instead of only once a week."

The new school was an instant success. The teacher's desk was an old packing case and the pupils sat on rough planks, but the mountain children came in such numbers that before long a new wing had to be added and an assistant hired to help the busy teacher.

Still Martha Berry was not completely happy. When school closed for the summer vacation, her pupils would quickly forget everything they had been taught. Often, too, during the school year, the boys would not show up for weeks at a time. "We need them for diggin' taters," their mothers would explain.

"What I should have is a boarding school," Martha decided, "where I can get these youngsters away from ignorance and misery, teach them not just reading and writing but cleanliness and good eating habits and modern farming methods. I could start with the boys. . . ."

That very day, Martha Berry drove into town and took the deed to the land her father had given her out of its safe-deposit box. Then she headed straight for the office of Judge Moses Wright, the Berrys' family lawyer.

"Judge Wright," she announced, placing the deed on his desk, "I want to transfer this property to my mountain boys. I'm going to start building a boarding school for them just as soon as I can."

"But Martha," the Judge protested, "once you transfer the rights to this property, you can never get them back. Since this is the only thing of value you own, I suggest you think this matter over very, very carefully."

"I have thought it over," Martha said firmly, "and if you are not willing to handle the transfer, then I shall find another lawyer who is."

Reluctantly Judge Wright recorded the transfer of the and to the new school which would open, Martha had decided, on January 13, 1902. "We have only two things to do before then," she said cheerfully, "build the school, and find some boys to fill it."

Once again Martha hitched up her horse and buggy and took to the woods. "I'm looking for boys," she told the folks she encountered along the narrow dirt paths, "boys who want some book learning and a chance to get ahead in life. The tuition is $50 but anyone who doesn't have the money can pay his way by working."

She had already hired a construction crew to begin building the new dormitory and when she was not off searching for students, she would stop by regularly to check on their progress.

"This is costing me every last penny I have in this world," she would remind them, "and I just want to be sure I'm getting my money's worth." The furnishings she assembled by ransacking the attic at Oak Hill and by begging castoff furniture from her neighbors. Once, hearing of an auction in Chattanooga, she hurried off and triumphantly returned with several dozen army cots that she had bought at a ridiculously low price.

The new school opened on schedule with the students as enthusiastic as their teacher. One boy, Clayton Henson, was anxious to become a lawyer. "How high can you carry me?" he wanted to know. "As high as you can go," was Martha Berry's reply. "Through the roof and up to the sky."

Another, Willie Jackson, walked thirty miles to get there leading his pig to pay for his "larnin'." Still another, Emory Alexander, brought a pair of oxen. "They're broke for plowin'," he announced, "and they're the fee for larnin' me."

Before the end of the year, Martha had enrolled eighteen boys and by the following spring one of them, Clayton Henson, was ready to graduate.

"You shall have the finest commencement we can manage," Martha promised him.

More than a hundred guests were invited to the ceremony and the town band agreed to provide music. As guest speaker, Martha boldly invited Hoke Smith, former Secretary of the Interior under President Grover Cleveland, later Governor of Georgia and a staunch advocate of the conservation of natural resources.

"That's why you should be interested in my school, Mr. Smith," Martha told him. "Boys are natural resources, too."

Although Hoke Smith was a busy man, Martha Berry was a determined woman. The only answer she would accept was yes and, worn down by her pleas, Smith finally agreed to come. Arriving at Mount Berry that evening, the guest of honor stared for a moment at the solitary barn-like building standing forlornly on the huge tract of land.

"Where is the school?" he said uneasily.

"Right here," Martha replied.

"And how many will receive their diplomas?" Smith asked.

"Only one," said the schoolmistress serenely, "and he's a fine boy—valedictorian and honor graduate as well."

The flabbergasted Mr. Smith had no choice but to mount the platform and deliver a stirring tribute to Martha Berry's school and to her first graduating class—Clayton Henson. Afterward, at Martha's insistence, he attended the young man's graduation party and, since the celebration lasted well into the night, remained overnight at the school's guest quarters.

As Hoke Smith told it later, his room was directly below a dormitory which housed twenty boys, most of whom stayed up all night laughing and talking. At 5 A.M., they arose and began packing their metal trunks, banging and bumping them all the way down the stairs. Each boy, as he passed Miss Berry's door, rapped loudly, and stopped to call out his thanks for a fine school year.

Exhausted and bleary-eyed, Smith finally emerged from his own room at 6. "Why, Mr. Smith," Martha declared solicitously at breakfast, "you've gotten up so early and you needed your rest."

The much-put-upon man, who was eventually to become a member of the school's board of directors, took out his checkbook. "Miss Berry," he said, "I am tremendously impressed with your need for more dormitories. Allow me to give you a small donation so you can get started on them at once."

The school could have used a dozen more such benefactors. Expenses, Martha soon found, were her biggest headache. She was constantly appalled at how much growing boys could eat. "Maybe I should have started with the girls," she sometimes thought. "I'm sure they'd be a whole lot cheaper to feed." Pots of beans and potatoes were forever simmering on the stove and at one meal she watched in horror as a ravenous mountain lad managed to consume an entire platter full of muffins at a single sitting.

"I know you're going to develop into a worthwhile citizen," Martha told him.

"How do you know?" replied the boy.

"Because all those good muffins just can't go to waste."

They didn't either. The boy grew up to be a state senator.

News of Martha Berry's school soon spread throughout the south and boys began drifting in not only from Georgia, but from Alabama, Tennessee and the Carolinas as well. No one was turned away even though each new pupil meant another set of textbooks, another bed and another mouth to feed.

One night as Martha was passing by the dormitory, she heard one of her boys talking to the Lord. "The dishpans are wearin' thin and the plowlines'll never last another year," he was saying. "I heard about some New York folks givin' money to schools. Dear God, give Miss Berry strength to get up there and tell them folks how much we need things. Amen."

By the end of the week, Martha Berry was on her way north armed with the names and addresses of everyone she could think of in New York who might be able to help her with her work. The first woman she talked to simply laughed. "Find yourself a nice beau and get married," she said. "Let some frump do things like this."

Another friend, more sympathetic, wangled her an invitation to speak at a Brooklyn church. Nervous and frightened, Martha nevertheless gave such a moving appeal for her boys that when she had finished, the members of the congregation came forward pressing bills into her hand and offering to send books and clothing and furniture to the school. One couple even jotted down the name of a prominent Wall Street financier.

"Don't tell him we sent you," they cautioned her. "But he is very generous and he might be willing to help."

Martha called upon the man who listened quietly while she told him about her school. "I was hoping," she said, "that you might give $50 to provide a scholarship for one of our boys."

"May I ask," the man said, "how much salary you receive?"

"Salary?" Martha said. "Why none—"

"Then what are you getting out of this?" the man wanted to know.

"I get a great deal," Martha told him vehemently, convinced by this time that the man had no intention of helping her. "I see boys come with only the clothes on their backs and go home to change the life around them. I watch them develop—"

While she was speaking the man wrote something on a piece of paper, folded it and handed it to her. Martha thanked him and left quickly. Not until she was outside did she open up the paper. There, instead of the $50 she had asked for, was a check for $500—scholarships for ten boys instead of only one!

After that first trip to New York, Martha was often on the go—Washington, Philadelphia, Baltimore, St. Louis, Chicago. "I will go anywhere and talk to anyone," she used to say, "as long as there is any chance of helping my boys."

On one occasion she even crawled out of a sick bed and struggled into her clothes in response to a phone call from an elderly man who said he wanted to talk to her about the school. When she arrived at the address he had given her, the man himself opened the door.

"Miss Berry," he said as soon as she had taken off her cape, "would you like to look at my elephants?"

"Oh, dear," Martha thought, "this is some kind of a practical joke and I am much too ill to find it very funny."

Aloud she murmured politely, "Of course."

Thereupon the man led her into the parlor and proudly pointed out his immense collection of carved ivory elephants. Martha had no sooner finished admiring them when the old man's sister appeared. "Now you must see my Japanese dolls," she said.

Still puzzled, Martha exclaimed over the delicate figurines.

"You are both very kind to show me all this," she said at last, "and I hope some day you will come to Georgia so I can show you my collection—of boys."

"Oh, yes," the man said, "I hear you have a splendid

school down there. Won't you come into the drawing room?"

When Martha had settled herself in front of the fireplace, the old man and his sister smiled warmly.

"Now I must confess," the man said, "this was a test. We thought that if you loved the school as much as we had heard, you'd come and be patient with two old folks tonight."

With that, he handed his astonished guest a check for $10,000.

Martha Berry's talents as a fund raiser had helped her conquer the biggest obstacle to the success of her school. But now that all was going well with the boys, it was time to tackle another dream.

"What we need," she announced to her board of directors, "is another school just like this one—only for girls."

"Impossible," cried one of the directors.

"Ridiculous," snorted another.

"It will mean another dormitory, more classrooms, books, food and money," still a third reminded her.

Undeterred, Martha returned to her office and began firing out a barrage of letters to educators all over the country asking for help in finding a woman who could direct "the most wonderful girls' school in the South."

After much correspondence she settled upon one woman who seemed ideally suited for the post.

"I am so anxious to see the new school," she said when Martha met her at the train.

"There it is." As they drove through the gates, Martha pointed to a clearing in the trees where some of the boys were just starting to work on the frame.

The new dean stared. "Can't you just see the girls?" Martha went on blithely. "We'll have ivy on the porches and violets along the paths. They'll love it."

"But where will we get the girls?" the woman stammered.

"We'll just go out and tag the bright ones," Martha told her, "exactly like we tag our trees for transplanting."

By Thanksgiving day in 1909 Martha Berry already had five girls enrolled in the school and by the end of the year there were twenty more.

The students were taught to plan and cook their own meals and to keep their dormitories tidy. The Singer Company, at Martha's request, donated a new sewing machine which the girls used to make all their own clothes. Martha also hired a crafts teacher and put them to work weaving shawls and bedspreads in the intricate patterns she had so often seen the mountain women use. Their handwork was exhibited at fairs all over the countryside where it served as a perfect advertisement for Berry Training and, incidentally, earned a tidy profit for the schools.

Play, however, was just as important as work. There were barbecues and songfests and, whenever one of the girls had a birthday, Martha insisted on having a party. So thrilled were the girls with this ritual that at one celebration the guest of honor refused to cut her cake. "Please cain't I have it around for a few days more," she begged, "ter see and ter admire. You know it's the first birthday I ever had and the first cake, too."

The board of directors had to concede that the addition of a girls' school was not the disaster they had predicted, and when, some years later, Martha suggested starting a college at Mount Berry, there was not even a murmur of dissent.

By that time, of course, Martha Berry's schools were the talk of the country. President Theodore Roosevelt had come to visit and been delighted with what he saw, and Andrew Carnegie had generously included Berry among his many charities. Perhaps the schools' closest friends, however, were Mr. and Mrs. Henry Ford. On their first visit to Mount Berry, the couple had been captivated by what Martha described as "a home-grown meal, a home-cooked dinner and a homespun school." There were many more visits after that. The auto manufacturer warmly approved of the Berry method of combining vocational training with academic studies. Ford, himself, spent happy hours tinkering with the schools' tractors and helping repair the farm machinery, while his wife, Clara, enjoyed watching the girls at their cooking and sewing.

Eventually, Ford sent his business manager around to look the place over and before he was finished the campus had been expanded with a collection of impressive Gothic buildings worth close to four million dollars.

Before her death in 1942, Martha Berry was showered with awards and citations. She became the first woman regent of Georgia's university system and the first woman member of the state's planning board. Universities flocked to present her with honorary degrees and in 1925 she was invited to the White House to receive the Theodore Roosevelt Memorial Medal for Distinguished Service from President Calvin Coolidge. Told she might invite five guests, Martha promptly chose five of her students. "They deserve this a lot more than I do," she told the President.

In spite of the worldwide recognition she received, however, Martha Berry's heart remained in the Georgia highlands. Until the very day she died, she was filled with hopes and plans for her schools and she avidly followed the careers of each of her graduates, honoring those who did especially well with a tree planted in their name on the Berry campus.

She was particularly pleased when one of her girls decided to marry one of her boys. The school chapel would be festooned with roses and smilax and Martha herself would give the bride away.

"I just love weddings," she used to say. "I remember when my five sisters got married in the drawing room at Oak Hill. I was a bridesmaid for every one of them."

"And you never had a wedding of your own?" a new bride once asked shyly.

"Why of course I did," Martha replied with a smile. "I just stepped across the road and married my schools. And just look at the thousands of wonderful children I've had."

NINE
✐ Florence Dunlop

Florence Dunlop stood in the center of the stage, her white
satin gown embossed with rich gold embroidery, her voice
clear and sweet as she sang the final notes of the aria. The
crowd roared its delight and scores of black-coated gentlemen in stiff white shirts rose to their feet shouting,
"Bravo!"

But before the radiant prima donna could even take a
bow, the spotlight glared straight in her eyes and a woman
who sounded strangely like her mother called, "Florence,
Florence. Have you forgotten what day it is? You'll be
late for the picnic!"

Blinking, Florence Dunlop rolled over on her back and
squinted up at the brilliant morning sunshine splashing
through the windows. A minute ago, she had been a world
famous opera star . . . now where was she?

"Oh," she squealed, suddenly remembering, "it's Dominion Day!" The dream forgotten, she leaped out of bed

and dashed into her sister Elsie's room. "Hurry up, sleepy-head," she called to the mound of rumpled bedclothes, "we're going on a picnic."

Elsie stirred lazily, then she, too, hopped out of bed. "I'll be ready in two minutes," she promised breathlessly.

Dominion Day was one of the Dunlops' favorite holidays. Commemorating the anniversary of the founding of the Dominion of Canada on July 1st, 1867, the day usually meant a family picnic on the edge of one of the lakes near their home in Rideau View near Ottawa, Ontario. Florence and her sister Elsie would help fix the sandwiches and hard-boiled eggs and their brothers would carry the heavy picnic hampers and the jugs of lemonade.

"I was having the most exciting dream when Mother called me this morning," Florence told Elsie as the two girls spread the flowered picnic cloth on the soft grass. "I was a famous opera star with my hair piled high on my head and a diamond tiara on top and a gorgeous white and gold gown. When I finished singing, people shouted, "Bravo! Bravo!""

"You do have a lovely voice," Elsie said excitedly. "Just think it might all come true some day . . . and I could sit in a box on opening night . . . and wear a long gown with a train and a feather boa . . ."

Forming a circle with the thumb and forefinger of each hand, Florence held them before her eyes and pretended to peer through a pair of opera glasses. "My dear," she exclaimed in haughty tones, "do look at that Florence Dunlop. Her face is every bit as lovely as her voice!"

Elsie giggled delightedly and Florence looked down at her plain gingham picnic dress and burst out laughing. "Goodness," she said, "I really do look like a prima donna today, don't I?"

Florence Dunlop never did become a world famous opera star and her sweet contralto voice was destined to be admired only at Sunday services when she sang with the United Church choir. She did, however, achieve greatness in quite a different way.

After graduating from high school, Florence Dunlop enrolled at Ottawa Normal School to become a teacher. "But teaching will be so dull, how can you ever stand it?" one of her schoolmates groaned.

"Dull?" Florence replied. "I don't think it will be dull at all. In fact, I have a feeling it may be a real adventure."

"An adventure?" the other girl hooted. "I can't imagine how anyone can make an adventure out of being a plain old schoolteacher!"

By the time she had completed her first week at normal school, Florence knew that her friend had been wrong. "Just helping boys and girls learn to read is exciting," she decided, "and that is only the beginning of a teacher's job." By the end of the second week she could hardly wait to get started in her new profession.

"How about a job as a rural teacher up in northern Ontario?" one of her professors suggested when she received her certificate in 1916. Florence liked the idea. "I have spent all twenty years of my life in and around Ottawa," she said. "It's time for a change."

The quiet countryside was indeed a change from Ottawa's busy streets and Florence quickly grew to love the thistle-dotted fields and brisk morning air. She was also amazed at how anxious the boys and girls seemed to be to make a good impression on their new teacher.

On her first day in the white wooden schoolhouse, she asked them about Samuel de Champlain and instantly the room was a sea of waving hands. "Suppose you tell us about him, Elizabeth," Florence said, choosing a tall girl near the back of the room.

"Samuel de Champlain was the founder and first governor of Canada," Elizabeth recited promptly.

"Very good," said Florence. "I can see from your faces that you've all learned that lesson, but I wonder how many of you know that Samuel de Champlain's wife started the first school in the country. Her students were Indian boys and she used a looking glass to entice them into the classroom. It was such a treat for the boys to see themselves in the mirror that they were willing to put up with a day of lessons to enjoy it."

The children laughed and a small boy in the front row raised his hand. "Please tell us some more stories, Miss Dunlop," he said. "Going to school is fun when you're the teacher."

The class was not always as eagerly attentive as they had been on that first day but Florence found them delightful nevertheless. One of the things that interested her most about the children was the vast difference in their abilities. "They are all the same age," she mused, "and yet Joseph has finished almost all of the problems in the arithmetic workbook while Mary Ann has barely memorized her times tables."

With reading it was exactly the same. One or two youngsters would far outdistance the rest of the class, one or two others would lag way behind. When she asked several of the more experienced teachers about it, they just shrugged. "It's always that way," one of them said.

As Florence continued in her work, she also began to realize that her pupils' personalities were just as varied as their scholastic abilities. Some were so quiet that it was all she could do to make them speak up in class; with others it was a struggle to get them to be still long enough to concentrate on their lessons. "I guess I must be terribly curious," Florence Dunlop decided, "but I just have to find out what makes them all tick."

After two years in the rural school system, Florence Dunlop decided to return to Ottawa. "I'm anxious to see if city children are very much different from their country cousins," she said.

It was a real pleasure for Florence to make her home once more in Canada's capital city. She loved to walk past the stately house where the Prime Minister lived and to see the Union Jack flying proudly in front of the Houses of Parliament. On Saturday afternoons, she would visit one of the museums or browse in the National Gallery and in the evenings go to the theater or a concert with a few of her friends.

The city children turned out to be just as lively and as

interesting as the rural youngsters had been and Florence was forced to admit that the real reason she had transferred to Ottawa was to satisfy her curiosity about all school-aged boys and girls. Enrolling for studies at Queens University, she was overjoyed to find professors who could explain, in part at least, exactly what makes children tick.

The more she taught the more Florence realized that her main interest was not really in the run-of-the-mill students, but in the unusual youngsters—the ones who found it hard to adjust to a regular school program simply because they were, in some way, different. There were those who were too bright, those who were too slow, the emotionally disturbed, the crippled, the chronically ill, the deaf and the blind.

"These are the ones I want to work with," Florence Dunlop declared, "the children who are special."

Already bursting with ideas of her own, Florence also devoured every educational magazine and psychological journal she could lay her hands on and when an opening was announced for an exchange teacher to work in London for a year, she quickly applied for the post.

"I'll be anxious to see how they cope with special education problems over there," she said.

Everything about the year abroad was an adventure— from the huge ocean liner that steamed down the St. Lawrence giving Florence Dunlop a magnificent farewell view of her homeland to the long Atlantic crossing with the porpoises playing in the ship's wake to her first glimpse of Buckingham Palace and the Houses of Parliament.

"Now I feel at home," Florence told her English guides. "Our parliament in Ottawa is exactly the same—right up to the clock at the top of the tower."

Florence visited Westminster Abbey, poked around the narrow streets in Kensington and gaped at the traffic swirling around Piccadilly Circus. But her first interest, as always, was her work. At the end of her year in London, she was offered a chance to do some more traveling, this time to South Africa, Australia and New Zealand where she visited schools, talked to teachers and studied programs for special pupils.

All the time Florence Dunlop was praying for an opportunity to put some of the ideas she was forming into practice in Ottawa's public schools. She returned home in the fall of 1927, full of enthusiasm for the project, and her prayers were answered when the city's Superintendent of Schools promptly named her Supervisor of Special Education.

"It's a big undertaking, Florence," he warned her, "and a pioneering one, too. We have never had an organized system of special classes in Ottawa before."

"Well, I've always found that the best way to handle any big job," Florence replied, "is to get to work on it right away."

By the end of the week, questionnaires had been sent out to every school principal in the city. How many children were having problems? What kind of problems? What were the children's names? Addresses? Dates of birth? Results of IQ tests? Reports of physical examinations?

The response was overwhelming. Every school had something to report . . . high IQ youngsters being deprived of the opportunity to forge ahead simply because the teachers had to give most of their time and attention to the average students, boys and girls with limited abilities struggling to keep up in an academic world which was obviously completely beyond them, children with weak eyes who could scarcely make out the words in their textbooks much less see what was being written on the blackboard, deaf youngsters unable to hear a single word the teacher spoke, boys and girls bedridden with chronic illnesses who might never be able to return to school.

The lights burned late in Florence Dunlop's office each night and Saturdays were no longer devoted to museums and concerts. "There is far too much work to be done," Florence told her friends.

Teachers had to be rounded up who could cope with special classes, doctors had to be consulted on a number of matters.

"What about children with heart problems?" Florence Dunlop would ask them. "How rigorous a schedule should they have? And tuberculosis cases—if we keep them outside a great deal of the time, can they get through a regular school day? Can we test the children's hearing and eyesight? What is the best way to go about it?"

Besides seeking the advice of local physicians, Florence Dunlop used her own talents as a trained psychologist to work out a system for the early identification and treatment of slow learners and another for identifying the bright students and accelerating their courses of study.

"My aim," she used to say, "is to give every child the best education possible—regardless of his abilities or handicaps."

The miracles, of course, did not begin overnight but gradually, year by year, Florence Dunlop worked out a complete system of special education aimed at every child in the city who was in need of help. There was a special class for emotionally disturbed students, a lip-reading class for deaf children, a sight-saving group for pupils whose vision was below par, sunshine classes for cardiac and crippled boys and girls and vocational schools for those who could not measure up in an academic atmosphere. For those children who were confined to their homes because of chronic illness, Florence Dunlop also organized a corps of visiting teachers who stopped by at regular intervals to keep them abreast of their school work.

But Florence Dunlop was more than just a very efficient supervisor. She was also deeply devoted to the children themselves and she considered it an important part of her job to keep in touch with their individual interests and needs. She was thrilled when a young blind boy told her of his excitement at joining a Boy Scout troop organized especially for his class and she treasured a mural depicting the discovery of Canada which a group of retarded youngsters had painted for her.

One of her favorite pupils was Larry, the victim of a serious automobile accident which had left him burdened with heavy braces and confined to a cumbersome wheelchair.

"When we organized a special class for crippled young-sters," she said, "Larry was one of the first pupils regis-tered. He graduated at the top of his class and went on to McGill University. Today he's a successful lawyer in Toronto and we're all very proud of him."

Another of her favorites was a pretty blonde girl named Isabel. "At first her teachers thought she was retarded," Florence explained, "but we gave her an IQ test and she did extremely well. It took a hearing test to unearth the real problem. Isabel was almost totally deaf. Right now, she is enrolled in one of our lip-reading classes and she is doing very well in her studies. We have also discovered that she is extremely talented at working with her hands. You should see the beautiful sweaters and scarves she can make."

Each June when she had cleared off her desk at the school board offices in Ottawa, Florence Dunlop would pack her bags and her books and head for New York City. There she attended Columbia University's summer sessions and eventually earned both her M.A. and her Ph.D.

"We've gotten so used to seeing you here in New York every year," the head of the psychology department told her, "we hope you'll continue with us as a regular member of the summer school faculty."

"I certainly will," Florence replied. "I always welcome the opportunity to spread the gospel of special education." Thus began an association that was to continue for the next eleven years.

Canadian teachers often called Florence Dunlop their

ambassador of good will. She traveled all over the world observing psychology clinics and special classes and lecturing on her own work in Ottawa. She was also one of a group of prominent educators who organized the International Council for the Study of Exceptional Children.

In the midst of her numerous professional activities, Dr. Dunlop also found time to lend a hand in the founding of Ottawa's Carleton University and to serve for many years as a lecturer in psychology at its evening sessions. "You must be exhausted by the time you get home at night," one of her students once said to her.

"Heavens, no," Dr. Dunlop replied. "One or two nights a week of seeing new faces and hearing new ideas keeps me alive mentally."

"But don't you ever take a vacation?" the student demanded.

"Of course," Florence Dunlop replied. "I take a holiday through my work."

A number of her work holidays centered around trips to the United States where she had become so well known in her field that cities all over the country were begging for her help in setting up special classes of their own. The United States Office of Education in Washington was one of the first to call upon her for advice and she subsequently served as a consultant in Maryland, Ohio and a number of California communities.

It came as no surprise to her admirers when, in recognition of her splendid work, President Dwight D. Eisenhower invited Florence Dunlop to attend the 1960 White

House Conference on Children and Youth. Dr. Dunlop refused to let even this tremendous honor interfere with her work. When a reporter for the Ottawa paper called upon her for an interview, he was told quite firmly that she was far too busy to see anyone. Only at the very end of the afternoon did she manage to squeeze in a ten-minute visit.

"But I really don't know what all the fuss is about," she protested. "I'm just doing a job that badly needs to be done."

By the time Florence Dunlop's sixty-fourth birthday rolled around, she had devoted nearly thirty years of her life to the Ottawa public schools. "Don't you think it's time to start thinking about retiring?" her sister Elsie suggested.

"Retiring?" Florence replied in amazement. "Why I don't feel any older than I did thirty years ago. How can I possibly think of retiring?"

There was a twinkle in her eye as she said it though, and she had already made plans for other equally well-trained teachers to follow in her footsteps. When she finally announced her resignation several months later, there seemed to be no end to the round of special dinners and luncheons in her honor.

"Well, Florence," said a well-wisher at one of the banquets, "now you're finally going to get the rest you deserve."

Dr. Dunlop chuckled delightedly. "I have no intention of resting," she told the solicitous gentleman. "What do you think I am—an old lady?"

The energetic white-haired teacher had already accepted a post as Professor of Special Education at San Francisco State College. "After all the years I've put into working and studying in this field," she declared, "it seems as if I have an obligation to pass along all the things I've learned to younger teachers. Let them carry on where I've left off."

Pleased as she was with her new life in California, Florence Dunlop still considered Ottawa her home. She chose to return there when, in the fall of 1962, San Francisco doctors gently informed her that her headaches and dizzy spells were not just signs of advancing age but symptoms of a serious and possibly fatal illness. A year later, Dr. Florence Dunlop was dead.

With characteristic modesty, she probably would have brushed away the lavish tributes that poured in from all over the world at the news of her death. "I can't see any reason to get excited," she probably would have said, "I'm only a plain old schoolteacher." A plain old schoolteacher who proved to be one of Canada's—and the world's—most dynamic educational pioneers.

TEN

⌒ℐ Virginia Gildersleeve

Whenever anyone asked Virginia Gildersleeve why she went to college, she would usually tell them, "I went to please my mother." Not many people believed her but it was the truth just the same.

Even as a first grader, Virginia had not been particularly enthusiastic about school. With two older brothers and a houseful of pets, staying home was much more fun than being cooped up in some stuffy classroom learning to add up a column of numbers.

The Gildersleeves lived in a roomy brownstone house on West Forty-eighth Street only a few steps from New York's Fifth Avenue. Today, this section is crammed with banks and shops and office buildings but in 1877 when Virginia Crocheron Gildersleeve was born, it was a quiet residential neighborhood that city dwellers from down by Stuyvesant Square or Astor Place considered the country.

The Gildersleeve children always had two or three dogs

and an assortment of rabbits, white mice, porcupines and snakes and when they grew tired of playing with their pets, there were glorious hide-and-seek games in the areaways between the brownstones. At dusk, they could dash upstairs to the front bedroom, pull aside the heavy lace curtains and watch the lamplighter go by.

On her first day at school Virginia Gildersleeve learned to read *It is a cat.* She was so pleased with herself at this accomplishment that she quickly raced through her entire reader and it was not long before she had her nose in every book in the family library—Dickens and Mark Twain and Chambers' Encyclopedia as well as dozens of the yellow-covered dime novels which her brothers were always bringing home.

"Come on out and play, Miss Bookworm," her brother Harry would say, playfully trying to drag her off her perch on the library couch.

"Um-m-m," Virginia would nod absent-mindedly. "Just let me finish this chapter."

Seven years older than Virginia, Harry had appointed himself her guardian almost from the minute she was born. He would often take her romping in Central Park and sometimes they would stroll over to Park Avenue to watch the New York Central trains come chugging along. Once when he was a student at Columbia University Harry had taken her on a visit to the university library.

"I have a few assignments to finish up," he explained. "Here is a book to keep you busy while I am working."

Virginia looked around at the green-shaded lamps and

the ceiling-high rows of books. "I like it here," she decided. Little did she dream that Columbia was to play a major role in her future.

At the end of the summer of 1891, Virginia Gildersleeve and both her brothers developed typhoid fever. Harry had a rather mild case and was up and about in a few weeks but Virginia's illness dragged on and she was still not completely well by the time her fourteenth birthday rolled around on October 3rd. To cheer up the listless invalid, her parents decided to give her a dainty gold watch from Tiffany's. Her brother Harry offered to make a presentation speech.

"To Miss Virginia Crocheron Gildersleeve on the fourteenth anniversary of her birth," he intoned with mock solemnity, "as a small token of the appreciation, regard and affection in which she is held by the entire family."

Hopping off the hassock from which he had delivered his oration, Harry grinned, bowed low and handed Virginia the slim red leather case.

"A gold watch!" she cried excitedly when she saw what it contained. "Now I have to get better so I can wear it."

No sooner had Virginia bounced out of her sickbed, however, than her beloved Harry was stricken with a relapse, developed a severe infection and died.

"At that moment," says Virginia Gildersleeve, "a black curtain cut my life in two."

The lively brownstone on Forty-eighth Street suddenly became a somber place with drawn shades and dim, lonely rooms. Mrs. Gildersleeve no longer gave teas or dinner parties and Virginia spent more and more time alone on the library couch with her books.

Harry had been one of the brightest students in his class at Columbia and had already embarked on a promising career as a lawyer. Hoping somehow to replace her brilliant son, the grief-stricken Mrs. Gildersleeve began taking a great interest in Virginia's education.

In January, after she had fully recovered from her bout with typhoid, the shy, sad teenager was enrolled at the Brearley School. Founded a few years earlier to prepare girls to pass the Radcliffe entrance examinations, Brearley prided itself on being a real no-nonsense institution. Extracurricular activities were unheard of and students were expected to learn etiquette and social niceties at home. School hours were reserved for German, French, Latin, mathematics and whatever other subjects could be crammed into the heads of adolescent girls.

It was the sort of program that a half-hearted scholar like Virginia Gildersleeve could not appreciate until years later. Nor was she especially responsive when, towards the end of her junior year at Brearley, Mrs. Gildersleeve began to talk about sending Virginia to college.

"You have the brains," she said firmly, "I don't see any reason why you shouldn't have just as good an education as your brothers."

The Brearley faculty had suggested Bryn Mawr as a suitable school but Mrs. Gildersleeve pooh-poohed the idea. "There is a perfectly good college right here in New York City," she told them.

A few years earlier in 1889, Columbia University had opened its own undergraduate division for women. Named in honor of one of the university's most dynamic presidents, Barnard College was at that time housed in an old brownstone mansion on Madison Avenue.

With her reluctant daughter in tow, Mrs. Gildersleeve descended upon the school. "Virginia would like to attend for a year or so as a special student in mathematics," she explained to the dean.

"We have no special students here," the dean informed them. "Everyone is required to take the full four-year course. There is also a complete set of entrance examinations."

As the dean proceeded to outline the subjects that would be included in the tests, Virginia breathed a huge sigh of relief.

"I haven't studied any Greek," she reminded her mother cheerfully as soon as they got outside. "I guess college is out of the question."

"Of course it's not out of the question," Mrs. Gildersleeve snapped. "We'll find a way to get you in."

Back at Brearley, Virginia was promptly enrolled in a special set of classes—including Greek—and from then on, her every waking moment was dedicated to the grueling job of preparing for the Barnard entrance examinations. At last, one muggy June morning, she mounted the steps at 343 Madison Avenue ready to put her newly accumulated knowledge on paper.

The mathematics section she found quite easy but then

arithmetic had always been one of Virginia's favorite subjects. After that came Roman history. "Give all the names
and dates of the Roman emperors," the first question read.

Racking her brain, Virginia came up with the first one—
Augustus. She thought maybe Tiberius had succeeded him
but after that her mind was a complete blank.

"I know I've failed," she thought glumly when the test
was finally over; but instead of being delighted that she
would not be able to go to Barnard, she found herself annoyed at her own stupidity. "Now I must go to college and
learn something," she decided.

But despite her ignorance of the Roman emperors, Virginia Gildersleeve did well on the rest of the examinations
and was accepted at Barnard. She entered on her eighteenth
birthday in 1895, a quiet, solemn freshman, still not completely resigned to her fate. Unimpressed with her classmates, she also disliked the shabby old house with its con-
verted bedroom classrooms and basement hall cloakroom.
At the meeting where class officers were being selected, she
sat all alone in the back row. "Well there's *one* person
sure not to be elected to anything," she thought mourn-
fully, "and that's VCG."

Miraculously, however, the sullen freshman gradually
blossomed into an eager student. She made several good
friends among her twenty-one classmates and the following year, VCG was elected president of the sophomore
class. Her devotion to the school was further enhanced by
the news that the detested Madison Avenue brownstone
was soon to be vacated and Barnard College ensconced on

a roomy campus adjacent to Columbia's newly established headquarters on Morningside Heights.

The girl who had gone to college to please her mother received her Bachelor of Arts degree from Columbia University in 1899. Mortarboard set jauntily on her head and sheepskin clutched in her hand, the new graduate was not only president of the Senior Class but its top scholar as well. Inside, however, she still felt a little like a frightened freshman. "Here I am educated," she thought to herself. "Now what?"

Virginia had not the slightest idea what, but since she had been awarded a scholarship for graduate study, she decided to enroll for her Master of Arts degree in history. At her next commencement, a year later, she was still no closer to deciding upon a career.

"Maybe I'll just take a year off and look around," she told her parents.

The Gildersleeves thought this was a very sensible idea. "You have been studying very hard," her father said. "I think you deserve a rest."

Virginia's rest ended abruptly a few weeks later when she received a note from Professor William Tenney Brewster of Barnard's Department of English. "We are going to have an additional class in English this year," he wrote. "Would you take over as instructor?"

Virginia was intrigued by the suggestion. "It might be fun," she mused, "to see what school is like from the opposite side of the desk."

And so Virginia Crocheron Gildersleeve became a

teacher and a very able one she was, too. So able, in fact, that Professor Brewster soon decided to promote her to teaching the entire course of required sophomore English.

Virginia declined politely. "I have decided to go back to school myself," she said. "I want to study for my Ph.D."

Back across the street to Columbia went VCG, back to assignments and examinations and term papers. By 1908, she was ready for still another commencement and with true femininity she was almost as excited about her new cap and gown as she was about the impressive degree she had earned. It was indeed a regal outfit—the handsome silk gown with blue velvet bands, the hood lined with Columbia's colors, sky blue and white, and the velvet mortarboard with its gold tassel. Dr. Virginia Gildersleeve was to wear it in academic processions for many years to come.

Returning to the Barnard faculty, Virginia Gildersleeve soon found herself in the midst of a bitter controversy. The dean's job was vacant and the Barnard trustees insisted that a woman should be appointed to the office. Columbia's president, Nicholas Murray Butler, was equally determined to find a man. Butler later backed down but by then it was almost impossible to find anyone to accept the post.

"What decent woman would want it?" one faculty member remarked. "She'll only be ground to atoms between the trustees and the president."

One afternoon, Virginia Gildersleeve received an ominous invitation to visit President Butler in his office at Columbia.

"Oh dear," she thought to herself, "I'm afraid I know what this is."

Nicholas Murray Butler lost no time in confirming her suspicions. "How would you like to be Dean of Barnard College?" he said.

"That depends on what the dean is going to do," Virginia replied decisively. "I have a very nice teaching position and I certainly don't want to give it up just to be a chaperone to the students. If I am going to be head of Barnard College, I want to have something to say about education."

President Butler was not making any promises but a few days later, he sent her a copy of the revised statutes of the college which granted the dean a whole range of new powers. Still Virginia hesitated. She loved teaching too much to give it up, yet she loved Barnard too much to see it ruined by some incompetent administrator. In the end, her devotion to the college triumphed and on February 1, 1911, Virginia Gildersleeve took office as Barnard's dean.

She was only thirty-three years old, an extremely youthful age at which to take on so much responsibility. On her first day in the big office at the northwest corner of Fiske Hall, she confesses that her only reaction was panic.

"I suppose I have to start sometime," she finally decided, getting a grip on herself. Pushing a button at the side of her desk, she called in her secretary and started tackling the problems of one of the country's foremost women's colleges.

"Years afterward," Virginia Gildersleeve recalled, "when

I began to drive a car, I had exactly the same sensation. I pulled or pushed or stamped on something. I had no idea what the result would be. It feels just like that when you begin being a dean."

Far from being ground to atoms between the trustees and the president, Barnard's new dean quickly proved to be in complete command of the situation. Scholarship became her primary concern.

"Make my girls work just as hard as your boys," she was constantly reminding the professors from Columbia who came over to teach at Barnard. She also instituted the custom of posting marks. "It's everybody's business whether a student has won an A or received a failing F," she used to say, "and knowing that it is makes a lot of girls work much harder."

"You won't believe it till you've tried it," she would prod the lazy ones, "but it's fun to use your mind."

Although discipline and conduct came under the jurisdiction of one of Dr. Gildersleeve's assistants, in the early years she herself was called in about a couple of crises which now seem rather amusing. One of them occurred the day the president of the school's Undergraduate Association shocked the Barnard community by walking across Broadway to Columbia without a hat; another was the uproar created in 1915 when the students participated in their annual spring games in bare feet.

Having grown up in New York City with its polyglot population of Irish, Italians, Slovaks and Germans, Virginia Gildersleeve was quick to appreciate the value of knowing people of other nationalities and backgrounds. She was always aiming for variety in Barnard's student body.

"Find me students of every economic, religious and social class," she used to tell her admissions officers. "Knowing and understanding different kinds of people is a valuable education in itself."

Dean Gildersleeve's own horizons stretched all the way around the world. Shortly after the First World War, she had helped establish the International Federation of University Women. Its purpose: "to promote understanding and friendship between the university women of the nations of the world and thereby to further their interests and develop between their countries sympathy and mutual helpfulness."

Through her work in international education, Barnard's First Lady made friends in England, Scotland, Hungary and Norway and even served on the Board of Trustees of the American College for Girls in Istanbul, Turkey. Her experiences abroad made her determined to bring the world back to Barnard. Through her urging the school developed a program for visiting professors. Women scholars from England, Spain, France, Germany and a host of other countries came to live for awhile on the Barnard campus and to conduct classes and seminars in their various fields.

Dr. Gildersleeve also pushed for the establishment of scholarships that would pay a student's room and board as well as her tuition. Generous friends quickly responded to her pleas and soon the college was welcoming young women from many distant points on the globe. "It is just as good for us as it is for them," Virginia Gildersleeve declared.

As a further boon to world understanding, Dr. Gildersleeve initiated a program of International Studies to enable advanced students to learn about the languages, literature, histories and cultures of many different countries.

The combination of her talents as a distinguished educator and an advocate of international good will made Virginia Gildersleeve the perfect candidate for a very important position.

One evening, in 1945, as she was taking a short rest before dinner, her housekeeper came to the door of her room.

"I want to be the first to congratulate you," she said. "It is a great honor."

"What is?" said Virginia Gildersleeve.

"Why, to be appointed a delegate to the San Francisco Conference," said her housekeeper. "I've just heard it on the radio."

Virginia Gildersleeve was so stunned that at first she refused to believe it; but sure enough, the following morning the newspapers listed the members of the United States delegation to the conference which would draw up the charter for the United Nations. Virginia Gildersleeve was the lone woman member.

Nor was Dr. Gildersleeve's fight for world understanding finished with the ratification of the United Nations Charter. Soon after she joined the United States Education Mission to Japan which had been invited by General

Douglas MacArthur to reorganize the defeated country's system of public schools.

There were hurried briefings by the State Department on the Japanese character and the prevailing educational theories, but none of them seemed quite as difficult to cope with as the official decree that she would not be allowed to fly over water in an army plane unless she was wearing slacks.

"But I've never owned a pair of slacks in my life," Virginia Gildersleeve protested.

"Sorry, Ma'am," came the response. "Orders."

After some frantic scurrying around New York's shops a pair of slacks was located and Virginia Gildersleeve went winging her way westward to the Orient.

It was no easy task for a group of American observers to attempt to change Japan's ancient educational traditions but they did suggest a number of ways of adapting them to the new political system of democracy. Their presence also went a long way toward boosting the morale of a conquered people at this low point in their history. One Japanese educator told Virginia Gildersleeve, "It is a kindly act you have done and we will never forget it."

Retired since 1946, Virginia Gildersleeve can look back on a lifetime of service to both her country and her college. Her career is remarkable proof that teachers, both in and out of the classroom, can be a marvelous source for good in our troubled world.